SOUNDS of the PASSION

SOUNDS of the PASSION

Meditations on Jesus' Journey to the Cross

David M. Owen

AUGSBURG Publishing House • Minneapolis

SOUNDS OF THE PASSION
Meditations on Jesus' Journey to the Cross

First North American edition published 1987 by Augsburg Publishing House, Minneapolis.

Original English edition published 1975 by Denholm House Press, Surrey, England, under the title *Sounds of the Passion*. Copyright © 1975 David M. Owen.

Scripture quotations unless otherwise noted are from the New English Bible. Copyright The Delegates of the Oxford University Press and The Syndics of the Cambridge University Press, 1961, 1970. Reprinted by permission.

Library of Congress Cataloging-in-Publication Data

Owen, David M., 1934-
    Sounds of the Passion: meditations on Jesus' journey to the cross
    David M. Owen.
       p.   cm.
    ISBN 0-8066-2298-9
    1. Jesus Christ—Passion—Sermons.   2. United Reformed Church in England and Wales—Sermons.   3. United churches—Sermons.
4. Sermons, English.   I. Title.
BT431.09 1987   87-28996
232.9'6—dc19   CIP

Manufactured in the U.S.A.   APH 10-5950

1 2 3 4 5 6 7 8 9 0 1 2 3 4 5 6 7 8 9

Dedicated to
MAURICE ROSCINI
my friend

CONTENTS

PREFACE

John Milton celebrated the birth of Jesus with his lively ode "On the Morning of Christ's Nativity," but failed to complete a companion piece on Jesus' death. A note was found appended to the incomplete beginning; "This subject the author finding to be above the years he had when he wrote it, and nothing satisfied with what was begun, left it unfinished."

Who, in attempting to explain Christ's death, does not share Milton's despair?

The cross is history's great paradox. It is the worst we know and yet the best. Never was there such hate, yet never such love—

> *From thence a paradox*
> *Which comforts while it mocks.*
> *Shall life succeed in that it seemed to fail?*

George Tywell faced many a hardship for Christ. "Again and again," he said, "I have been tempted to give up the struggle, but always the figure of that strange Man hanging on the cross sends me back to my task again!"

I pray the same purpose be served through this book. It may be that, as we follow the drama of this "week of weeks," we shall associate ourselves with the characters in it—their hates and fears, hopes and loves. May it be, above all, that in hearing the "sounds of the passion," we shall identify ourselves more closely with this Jesus, and be better able to serve him in our day.

DAVID MALDWYN OWEN

Reigate, 1974

ACKNOWLEDGMENTS

The author thanks the publishers concerned for permission to quote from the following:

Church Missionary Society:
Bengal Bishop .... R. Bryan

Gill and Macmillan Ltd:
Prayers of Life ....M. Quoist

David Higham Associates Ltd:
The Man Born to Be King ....Dorothy L. Sayers

Hodder and Stoughton Ltd:
Rhymes .... G. A. Studdert Kennedy

H. G. Wells Estate:
Extract on page 83

The Society of Authors, as the literary representative of the Estate of John Masefield:
The Trial of Jesus

SCM Press Ltd:
Contemporary Prayers
  for Public Worship .... ed. Caryl Micklem
Meditations on the Cross .... Toyohiko Kagawa

1

THE SHOUT
of the CROWD

Meanwhile the chief priests and elders had persuaded the crowd to ask for the release of Bar-Abbas and to have Jesus put to death. So when the Governor asked, "Which of the two do you wish me to release to you?," they said, "Bar-Abbas." "Then what am I to do with Jesus called Messiah?" asked Pilate; and with one voice they answered, "Crucify him!" "Why, what harm has he done?" Pilate asked; but they shouted all the louder, "Crucify him!"
Matthew 27:20-22

Sometimes they strew his way,
And his sweet praises sing;
Resounding all the day
Hosannas to their king.
Then "Crucify!"
Is all their breath,
And for his death
They thirst and cry.

I

"The voice of the people is the voice of God."

"Might is right."

"God is on the side of the big battalions."

In other words, if the majority are for it, it must be right.

When the two candidates were put to the vote, the matter was decided "nem con." Who would dare to oppose, anyway, for these were not the days of free speech? It was safer to go with the crowd than take a stand on principle.

A few days before it was easy to do so. As the procession moved through the streets of Jerusalem, the crowds went wild with excitement;

"Hosanna to the Son of David! Hosanna in the highest!"

It's an expression we have over-sentimentalized—

> To whom the lips of children
> Made sweet hosannas ring.

But in this Hebrew cry for deliverance there was little sweetness: *Hoshach-na*—"Save us, we pray!" Many were inciting to rebellion against their Roman aggressors, and were sure Jesus was the one to lead it.

There was an abnormal crowd at the time which swelled the everyday population of Jerusalem well beyond its usual size. The great feasts, particularly the Passover, meant an influx of Jews not only from Judea but also from the provinces beyond, and, according to Josephus, some 2,700,000 people would throng the city. They held deep religious convictions, and the "City of David" was the center of all they held dearest. Emotions ran high. At every turn were stark reminders of alien occupation as the Roman military mingled with the crowds. The governor usually attended the Passover feast himself, but even he must have felt insecure at the prospect of a national uprising. It is a testimony to Roman skill in administration that for 60 years at least the Roman procurators in Judea had managed to avert any serious trouble. Their danger lay in a popular leader.

After the triumphal entry no one was more popular than Jesus. Patriotic nationalism does this to a man, as our bloodstained history reminds us. Some of the rottenest and most cruel deeds have been wrought in its name. Once inflamed it stops at nothing. It smashes democracy; it stifles reason and conscience; it deprives man of his humanity and makes him a monster; it crucifies the noble.

Ronald Blythe tells how the Hitler youth were intoxicated by their new leader. He writes in *The Age of Illusion:* "When they wheeled by the box containing Göring, Goebbels, and Hitler, the Führer screamed, 'Heil, mein Arbeitsdienst!'—and received in reply a shout of devotion."

The popular man is impregnable whilst his popularity lasts—shielded by the fortress of acclaim. The mob would have lynched any man that day who had dared to suggest Jesus should die. They were there, but as observers only—to see what he would do. Some had not given up hope that he might yet turn out to be the longed-for Messiah. So a lot of people had a vested interest in him at that moment.

It was a severe test for Jesus—for everyone enjoys a measure of popularity. He had faced a similar test at the start of his ministry. To demonstrate his unique

15

ability by turning stones into loaves, and walking away unharmed after jumping from the top of the temple, would have got the masses flocking after him—the hungry, the under-privileged, the sign-seeker—all sorts. His own oppressed people needed him badly, and the time seemed right for daring leadership. With public opinion so much on his side, what more could a man want? And with death around the corner waiting to judge irrevocably his chosen way, he might have been excused for changing his tactics.

But he had thought it all out. He warned his disciples that he was going to Jerusalem to die. He had planned this event as well as he had planned that supper in the upper-room. Pilgrims were expected to enter the city on foot, but he rode; furthermore, the animal he chose had deep significance. The "colt" was clearly to be understood not as a young war-horse but as the symbolic and sacred "ass's foal" on which the Messiah was expected to ride. It was a deliberate gesture intended to alert those who could interpret it to the fact that he was himself the promised Messiah. And when he rode on the "beast of peace" through the shouting mob and into the temple, to overthrow the tables of the religious profiteers, there was no mistaking his intentions. His fellow countrymen expected he would denounce their oppressors and lead them to freedom. Not so. Not a word against the Romans, but for the Jews, an outburst of indignation.

Small wonder they turned against him. It all looked so hopeful; now they had to resign themselves to yet another disappointment, to yet another abortive claim to liberty.

"Give us Bar-Abbas" they shouted.

16

.

Dorothy L. Sayers describes Bar-Abbas: "It does not do to think of him as just a 'robber' or a 'murderer'—we must think of him as a member of the I.R.A., arrested during the 'troubles'; with Jesus as the rival candidate presented by the English governor-general for the kindly consideration of a Dublin crowd." Beside this rebel the gentle appeal of Jesus seems ludicrous. He had been imprisoned for his part in a rising against the Romans, and for murder. Given his way he would show no mercy on the enemy. But Jesus had said, "Love your enemies and pray for your persecutors."

The Jews were quick to seize upon a custom of releasing a prisoner at Passover, so who better now than Bar-Abbas? His credentials were promising.

"Then what am I to do with Jesus called Messiah?" asked Pilate.

And with one voice they answered, "Crucify him!"

II

A crowd is like that. A man individually may be resolute and resistant; put him in a biased mob and as often as not these qualities evaporate. Bombard him with slick slogans, whip him up into mass hysteria, and the cause is won—the biggest rogue is crowned a prince.

Crowd behavior is a fascinating study, and we have more opportunity than any previous generation of pursuing it. Crowds are becoming inescapable almost everywhere, and as world population increases, so has society to gear itself to meet its clamorous demands. So easily can quality be sacrificed in the interests of quantity.

Let it be said—the church today, apart from occasional mass evangelistic rallies, has little experience of crowds. At one time it was necessary to erect large church and chapel buildings to accommodate the masses eager for religion. What the churches did with the crowds they once had is a 50 years story, and what they must do with the crowds that never enter their doors, is today's challenge.

Crowd appeal is immensely strong. A large congregation is inspiring to both worshiper and preacher, and nothing is more discouraging to both than a building that displays more wood than people. The spasmodic churchgoer hardly understands how much his absence damages the witness of the church. Whether in church or in the street, nothing draws like a crowd. It creates excitement. It means something is either happening or is about to happen.

Certainly, it has its good qualities. A crowd guarantees a measure of security. "Safety in numbers" is a meaningful cliché in the setting of democracy. But on frequent occasions the minority are not always silent. Sometimes they threaten and plunder until the majority become the silent sufferers. Sometimes a whole country is held to ransom by the militant strategies of a few; indeed, we are seeing as never before that the activity of uncontrolled minorities can lead to anarchy. So a crowd moved in the right direction is a useful safeguard.

And there is comfort in a crowd. When animals normally at each other's throats are in danger from fire or flood, they are said to herd together amicably.

We humans, also, are never more gregarious than when faced by a common danger, as when during the blitz in Britain in the Second World War, people in communal air-raid shelters and underground stations threw differences and inhibitions to the wind.

But all good qualities aside—*a crowd is potentially dangerous,* as the days following Jesus' arrival in Jerusalem showed. For as the fashionable winds blew and altered course, so the virtues of dignity and self-control were scattered as chaff before them. So was the virtue of loyalty, for it paid them to support the other side when the chips were down. They were like the shopkeepers in Jordan who openly exhibited patriotic pictures of King Hussein, making sure that under the counter were also pictures of President Nasser, should they be needed!

It was this crowd, like every crowd—prone to fickleness—that sent Jesus to his cross. The time was too pregnant with emotion, and sensitive hopes too quickly raised, for sound judgment to prevail. His way seemed so futile, and they wanted none of it.

III

This did not surprise Jesus in the least, for he knew about crowd behavior, which is noteworthy in a religious leader. Rita Snowden says: "Our Lord spent a lot of time with the crowds. Hitherto, religion had lived much in the temple of abstract thought, in pleasant seclusion, sought after by those in need. But this was not our Lord's way."

The Gospels tell us that Jesus was frequently in the midst of the great crowds that followed him; he spoke to them and had compassion upon them. He once showed his capacity for leadership in organizing a multitude of several thousand people to sit in neat rows so as to give them food. He was one religious leader who had a way with crowds. When he addressed them, the learned were stimulated by his wisdom while the common people heard him gladly. We get some idea of the following he must have had by the despair of the Pharisees; "You see," they say to one another, "you are doing no good at all; why, all the world has gone after him!" He loved the crowds that thronged him yet he would never pander to their every wish. "Give us a sign," they demanded. He did, but not what was expected.

Just how does he regard our banner-waving, slogan-chanting age? So much would cause him pain; so many demands for "my rights," so much anger and intolerance. But some protesting could well meet with his approval.

People are beginning to care more than ever about what they regard as evils in today's world, and are venting the shame they feel. They are sick of war; of so-called justified wars; sick of nuclear stockpiling that mocks human enterprise; sick of racial injustice and inequality, and of the appalling division of our world into the "haves" and the "have-nots." They are sick of the pollution of land, sea, and atmosphere, and equally sick of the pollution of the mind by verbal and literary filth. And what needs to be noticed in this growing volume of protest is that young people are much in evidence, and they have a right to be so. True, we don't care much for the demeanor of some "off-beats" found among demonstrations; nevertheless they could be saying something of importance in the only way they know how; indeed, God speaks more often than we care to admit, through unorthodox and unseemly ways!

You can be sure Jesus understands, and that where encouragement is justified, he gives it. He is not offended by the hordes of youths who noisily claim him as their champion, and hail him "superstar." He's been through it all before—as on the road into Jerusalem.

To understand does not mean to give way to every demand. Jesus saw a deeper need which cried for fulfillment.

It is recorded that on one occasion he saw a great crowd and "his heart went out to them, because they were like sheep without a shepherd"—harassed and helpless.

Souls of men, why will ye scatter
Like a crowd of frightened sheep?

His understanding is the same—always. His heart went out to that irresponsible crowd who sent him to his death. They were mostly strangers to each other, yet so much passed between them; many would not have known what they were shouting about anyway—so he would have prayed forgiveness for their ignorance.

And with equal compassion does he look upon our present-day crowds.

Modern life is in great danger of becoming impersonal and insensitive. In spite of our progress towards peace, racial harmony, and social justice, we are finding it harder to love the individual. Indeed, it is subtly possible to love all men in general and no one in particular—as Zossima pointed out in Dostoyevsky's novel *Brothers Karamazov*.

Our cities are crammed and overflowing; our towns are growing to the size our cities used to be, and the hitherto peacefulness of our village life is threatened with "overspill." Everywhere crowds are staking their claims upon a shrinking land and an already strained society, and with it all goes the danger of depersonalization. Nowhere is an individual more lonely than in a crowd—in a crowded city where people jostle each other continuously yet rarely meet. Who can tell the amount of loneliness in that crowded commuter train or lunch-hour restaurant?

The problem is posed, though in a different setting, by the Viennese psychologist Bruno Bettelheim who was imprisoned as a Jew in Buchenwald during the last war. He studied closely the process of depersonalization at work in the overcrowded concentration camps. The camp guards, the S.S., and the prisoners alike soon learned to regard each other as "replicas of a type," in much the same way as an anatomist may regard the human body he is dissecting. Bettelheim observed that this was really done in self-defense, for it shielded them from the responsibility of having to treat each other as persons to be cared for—people with identities.

It is not only in the brutality of a war-time situation that we see this at work. It is happening today and will go on happening in the clamorous world of spreading cities and massive business.

All around us then—"the madding crowd's ignoble strife."

IV

"Jesus would have us learn that a crowd is nothing more, nothing less than a gathering of persons with distinctive identities."

22

Someone coined the phrase, "revolving doors cutting crowds into people." And this was Jesus' method.

When a woman in a crowd touched his cloak, his disciples thought it odd that he should ask who had touched him. But this was different. It was a touch of great need and urgency. He is speaking to a crowd when someone interrupts for advice on some personal problem—perhaps a family squabble, or, more often, a cry for healing. Invariably he diverts his attention to that particular need. Why in such a crowd should he notice a little man perched up a tree, or a widow weeping for her son, or why pay attention to one leper or one blind man—for weren't they everywhere?

But he was that kind of Christ. He never would let a man get lost in a crowd or shrink from his responsibility.

Today is the computer age, and we treat people "en masse." We stick labels on them—they are supporters of this cause or members of that denomination, and are named accordingly; or they are "cases" or "clients." But Jesus will have none of it. In his eyes, souls are never carbon copies, and he loves each one of us as if there was only one of us to love. Francis Thompson's lines well befit his outlook:

> *There is no expeditious road*
> *To pack and label men for God,*
> *And save them by the barrel-load.*

And our Lord is an example and a warning to us all. Through his experience we see what a man is like in and out of a crowd—what he can do, what a mob can do—its strength and weakness. At Passiontide we walk with him, if we dare, along the clamorous route into the city and beyond, to hear the shout of the crowd—derogatory, cruel, ignorant. Yet he could only love them—to a man. They gave their verdict against him, but he went on to save them.

Lord Jesus Christ—
When the people's praises turned to jeering and they shouted, "Crucify!" you prayed for their forgiveness. Lord Jesus, we know that we are the same sort of people as those who jeered at you then: we too need your forgiveness.
Contemporary Prayers for Public Worship

2

THE SOUND
of WEEPING

Daughters of Jerusalem, do not weep for me; no, weep for yourselves and your children.   Luke 23:28

> *Thus might I hide my blushing face,*
> *   While his dear cross appears;*
> *Dissolve my heart in thankfulness,*
> *   And melt my eyes to tears.*
>
> *But drops of grief can ne'er repay*
> *   The debt of love I owe;*
> *Here, Lord, I give myself away;*
> *   'Tis all that I can do.*

I

"Tears," said Voltaire, "are the silent language of grief."

We accept children's tears as a part of their growing up, but tears in an adult tell of a deeper grief and call for warm understanding. On the other hand, there are tears that call not so much for compassion as restraint, for is it not true to say that the gentle and inescapable persuasion of a woman's tears have sometimes won where weapons and politics have failed? Byron voices what many a man has known—and often failed to resist:

> *Oh! too convincing—dangerously dear—*
> *In woman's eyes the unanswerable tear!*
> *That weapon of her weakness she can wield,*
> *To save, subdue—at once her spear and shield.*

But there was one dramatic moment when their appeal found no response, and their sympathetic gesture rebounded.

Luke alone gives us the story of the weeping women of Jerusalem—and how it typifies his gospel in which women have a very special place! Someone observed that of all those who opposed Jesus, not one woman is found among them. This may have been due at the time to their inferior social status. To this day certain Jewish males in their morning prayers thank God that they have not been born a woman! But Luke gives us a different picture of Jesus than was current in his day. While rabbis ignored women— even their own wives—in public, the "rabbi" Jesus was known to talk with them openly. He seemed to befriend all sorts—racial enemies, Gentile misfits, and even moral reprobates. Women the world over owe him so much, if only as the instigator of their liberation movement! Nor can it be overlooked that history's greatest event—the resurrection of Jesus Christ—was first made known to a woman. The story of Mary Magdalene weeping at his tomb, and how

Jesus spoke to her, is among the loveliest ever recorded.

A woman's tears may bring out the best or the worst in men. They may win where other means have failed. They have potency enough "to pierce into a marble heart." Yet when some Jerusalem women wept over Jesus it was in vain:

"Weep not for me," he told them, "no, weep for yourselves. . . ."

Does that sound hard and ungrateful of him? After all, it was the only language they had at that moment, and it was surely a welcomed contrast to the others who were clamoring for his death. So why refuse their tender sympathy? Why increase the anguish of those already in deep sorrow by telling them they ought to weep for themselves instead?

The Gospels tell of occasions when he was deeply moved by people's distress. He knew the sorrow of a father for his sick daughter, of a widow for her dead son, of a sister for her brother. Compassion was the hallmark of his ministry, not just in wordy sympathy but in real involvement. When news of Lazarus's death reached him, John says: "Jesus wept." Grief is the most heartrending experience of all, but to know that he too suffered this "aching void" is to draw us to him at the moment of our own pain:

> *In every pang that rends the heart,*
> *The Man of Sorrows has a part.*

Jesus wept. He wept for his beloved city through which he had passed for the last time; the city that had stoned the prophets and now had condemned him. He had spoken of the sorrows that would accompany him. He had told his disciples that he would cause them to weep and mourn. Why then reject this gesture of sympathy for himself in his own anguish?

II

Did he think it was not genuine, only another of those ostentatious displays so customary in a time of bereavement?

Public mourning among Jews was a noisy affair. Death was announced with loud shrieks. Neighbors were invited to the house to lament, and mourners were sometimes hired to help maintain the emotional pitch. Burial usually took place within 24 hours, throughout which the weeping and wailing went on; the more unrestrained the greater the respect—or so it was felt. The Wailing Wall of Jerusalem is a reminder to this day that no one can weep quite like the Jew.

But Jesus would have no illusions. Don't we feel his impatience with those noisy mourners in the house of Jairus—"Why this crying and commotion?" No, anything showy and shallow would quickly meet his disapproval. Byron reflected on "tears which women shed and use at their liking"—the sort that would leave Jesus unconvinced.

But this surely was genuine. Publicly to mourn a criminal on his way to execution was unlawful, and so punishable. They must have known their weeping could cost them dearly, so it was a most courageous thing to do.

It is suggested that they were weeping from guilt. Were these women among the crowds who first acclaimed Jesus, and then, like the rest, turned against him? Are they now weeping with remorse? Scarlett O'Hara in *Gone with the Wind* exclaims: "Oh, it seemed so right when I did it, but it was all so wrong. If I had to do it over again, I'd do it so differently." Did they feel like her—burdened with a longing to make amends? Is this their way of saying "sorry"—an act of confession that alone can assuage their guilt?

Jesus would understand and forgive—as always, but they have to bear the responsibility for their behavior. He is condemned and on his way to the cross, and nothing can reverse the verdict against him. They have reason indeed to mourn him as one already dead.

III

Paradoxically, the women's gesture of sympathy was the last thing that Jesus wanted. This is a key reason why he rejected it. Some people thrive on pity. They are never content unless bemoaning their mishaps and expecting someone to share their self-pity. They are most difficult to befriend. Thankfully, there are also the selfless ones who will take no pitying however cruel a blow has been dealt them.

There was Thomas Carlyle. Having completed the first volume of his work on the French Revolution, he gave the manuscript to his friend John Stuart Mill to read. Mill's housemaid, seeing what she thought was a bundle of wastepaper lying on his desk, threw it all on the fire. With no record kept of his arduous research, Carlyle had to start all over again. Still, he would have no one lament his misfortune; "Do not pity me," he said, "but forward me rather as a runner that though tripped down, will not lie there, but tip and run again." Sir Walter Scott was a wealthy man until the printing and publishing firms in which his whole fortune was invested, went bankrupt. "But people," he said, "will not dare to talk of me as an object of pity . . . adversity is to me at least a tonic and a bracer."

Francis Thompson speaks of "ills that we do in tenderness." There is a sentimentality which can prove as dangerous as violence. The Passion story has all that is needed to move the hardest heart to tears, but let pity get misdirected and it becomes a stumbling-block. "Behold, and see if there is any sorrow like unto my sorrow"—are words commonly associated with our Lord's passion. But they are not his words. Countless hymns and sermons, too, have been aimed at converting men by his sorrows; but from his remark to these weeping women it seems unlikely that he would approve.

> Weep not for him who onward bears
> His cross to Calvary;
> He does not ask man's pitying tears,
> Who wills for man to die.

The real appeal of the cross is in its gesture of extremity. No man's love is greater than when it is laid down for others; beyond this, love cannot go. Jesus, on his way to the cross, will not have himself pitied as a victim who would, given half a chance, escape from what lies ahead. It is his will to die—"I am laying it down of my own free will," he said. Nothing is more out of place than pity for one who does that. "Do not weep for me" is therefore a word of stern rebuke.

And we need that rebuke, for it is subtly possible to follow him for the wrong reasons. He reminds us here that we are never to think of enlisting in his service if it is out of sentiment or benevolent patron-age. A woman once told me that she attended the Sunday evening service in her church purely out of sympathy for her minister whom she pitied having to preach to so few! Those of us who preach will doubtless appreciate the loyalty of her kind. At least she was honest, but really her pity was misdirected.

It illustrates the point. Jesus cherished loyal friendship. When the crowds were deserting him he asked his disciples with, one feels, a longing for their continued friendship, if they also wanted to leave him. When Peter asserted their renewed allegiance, Jesus immediately put discipleship in its right per-spective. "Have I not chosen you?" he asked them.

Make no mistake—he is in command always. He calls us to be fellow workers, and this is the wonder of the call, *but in no way does he require sympathetic encouragement.* His kingdom's cause is not a charity. He chooses to bring about his grand purpose through men, but if we fail him, he is still not defeated. When the women sobbed for him as a broken victim, they failed to see that he was on his way to victory.

I have known the church to pander to this pa-tronistic mood. It is generally thought to be the par-son's job to get people to "support" the church. Con-sequently the church has acquired a depraved image of "support techniques," as a means of propping up a cause that would otherwise collapse—which all seems to make mockery of the stupendous concept of the church of Pentecost. The gospel committed to us is a pearl above price, and far too precious to be demeaned by substandard practices. But the church commits this sin time and time again. It gives the tragic impression that the cause of Christ is obsolescent and that he must be weeping from self-pity at the thought.

We must know that *everything is for his sake*. With that formula we end most of our prayers; we say, "for the sake of Jesus Christ." It is an affirmation that roots and directs our faith, but it bears no hint of patronism. Jesus Christ wills his church to continue here not for his own possessive pleasure. What we do "for his sake" is not as some who once offered gifts to please and appease their gods. No, we are not his patrons, nor does he cry for himself should we fail him.

If present church statistics are anything to go by, the cause of Christ is in bad shape. So what do we do? Do we compromise so as to make the gospel less demanding, and, we hope, more appealing? If the church is so unpopular have we any right to expect much commitment from those who are members of it? Would it not be better condescendingly to accept what spare time they may have to lend a hand? How much of an "optional extra" has the church become, and just how much debased activity and sloppy sentiment goes into the running of it? I know one church that has been dying for years. It was once useful to the Lord. Now the handful of those who are not so elderly are propping up the cause for those who are, and who would be upset to see it close. We must understand, but there is a price on our understanding. The time has run out for sentimentally prolonging the failing health of church buildings whose purpose has been served.

But we Christians do not belong to a dying cause. We have no reason to weep and every reason to rejoice.

The changing fortunes of the church here do not indicate that Jesus Christ is at last on his way to defeat, or even that God is dead—as some have thought. Though membership statistics depress and church buildings crumble, Christ's work goes on. Our appeal to men is not so much to support the church as to serve the kingdom, and supporting and serving are rather different in meaning.

IV

"Weep not for me, but for yourselves."

"For yourselves"—this has the force of a rebuke. He is not calling for tears of self-pity but for tears of repentance; tears that show a willingness to bear responsibility and the consequence of the evil that is being done.

Michel Quoist has this in mind:

> I manage very well, Lord, to pity your sufferings and the
>   sufferings of the world.
> But to weep for my own sins, that's another matter.
> I'd rather bemoan those of others,
> It's easier. . . .
> I've found plenty of guilt . . . in many others, Lord, many
>   others.
> All in all, in just about the whole world, except me.

Jesus insists on putting responsibility where it belongs—on you and me. Had these women had an opportunity they had let slip? Were they silent when they should have spoken out? Were they, like the rest, swayed by changing opinions? Had they forgotten all that Jesus had done and doubted what he could yet do? These were reasons deep enough for tears.

And their failure had brought with it devastating consequences beyond themselves. They are to weep for that for which he wept on his way into Jerusalem.

"When he came in sight of the city, he wept over it and said, 'If only you had known, on this great day, the way that leads to peace! But no; it is hidden from your sight. For a time will come upon you, when your enemies will set up siege-works against you; they will bring you to the ground, you and your children within your walls, and not leave you one stone standing on another, because you did not recognize God's moment when it came.' "

Their failure to recognize "God's moment" and to act upon it, had rendered them the victims. They have brought God's judgment upon themselves.

Jesus says to them: "The days are coming when they will say, 'Happy are the barren, the wombs that never bore a child, the breasts that never fed one.' Then they will start saying to the mountains, 'Fall on us,' and to the hills, 'Cover us.' For if these things are done when the wood is green what will happen when it is dry?"

In Judea a childless marriage was a tragedy. But Jesus is saying that the day would soon come when the woman without a child would be fortunate. And if this should happen when the nation is prosperous, what will happen when its life has withered? These are hard words, and their right interpretation is not clear, yet there seems little doubt that they are prophetic of the impending catastrophe which was gruesomely fulfilled during the Jewish rebellion against the Romans in A.D. 66–70.

And it is a warning to heed. William Penn said that men must choose to be governed by God, or they condemn themselves to be ruled by tyrants. Jesus Christ is decisive for men and nations, and these Jerusalem women had to learn, as all of us have to, that deciding what to do about him is a crucial and an agonizing thing, and that far from him being a broken victim whom we mourn, he strides ahead as conquerer and king.

James Russell Lowell reminds us of that moment of decision which comes "to every man and nation," and which, as he sees it, is always a decision about Christ:

> By the light of burning martyrs,
> Christ, thy bleeding feet we track
> Toiling up new Calvaries ever
> With the cross that turns not back.

Let us be sure our tears are well directed.

Lord, thou goest forth alone to thy sacrifice: thou dost offer thyself to death, whom thou art come to destroy. What can we miserable sinners plead, who know that for the deeds that we have done thou dost atone? Ours is the guilt, Lord: why then must thou suffer torture for our sins? Make our hearts so to share in thy passion, that our fellow-suffering may invite thy mercy.

Peter Abelard

3

THE CROWING
of the COCK

Peter said, "Man, I do not know what you are talking about." At that moment, while he was still speaking, a cock crew.   Luke 22:60

I

"Cock-sure" we say. And he is.

The cock is a paragon of conceit and brazen-faced impudence. Self-assured, pugnacious—he tolerates no rival.

"As sure as the cock is to crow in the morn"— and few things are surer. He never sleeps late. He is said to crow every morning of his life. Muslims believe that when the cock ceases to crow the day of judgment is at hand.

Shakespeare's Horatio speaks of the cock as "the trumpet to the morn." In classical mythology he is dedicated to Apollo the sun god because he announces the rising of the sun; to Mercury the god of skill because he summons men to their business by his crowing, and to Aesculapius the god of medicine because "early to bed, early to rise, makes a man healthy. . . ."

Admire his confidence, dislike his arrogance—he is a bird to be reckoned with. He has always commanded man's attention—sometimes dramatically.

A writer tells of his experiences in a German P.O.W. camp during the last war. He recalls how he and a fellow prisoner brought off a daring escape during one night. Once outside the camp they ran for miles without stopping until, at last, exhausted, they slumped into dense undergrowth. He remembers the agony of blistered feet, of pain-racked bodies, of the chilly, damp surroundings, and the intense fear. He must have dozed for a while for he was startled into reality by a crowing cock. In those bewildering moments he sensed the thrill of at last being free. But with equal suddenness and as a spur to vigilance, came the sickening awareness that his "freedom" was only half true. He was still a prisoner in a hostile country, and, no doubt, the worst struggles lay ahead.

The crowing cock must not be ignored.

Another man, Simon Peter, needed freedom badly. He was implicated with a condemned prisoner, Jesus of Nazareth, and he was in dire trouble. So to extricate himself, integrity went overboard. Though he had been Jesus' righthand man for three years, he now swore that he never knew him.

And he got away with it. His accusers, it seems, never reported their suspicions and no action was taken against him. It was a near thing, but he had made it. He was free at last, or so he thought, until the crowing cock shattered his make-belief and faced him with the awful truth.

Jesus was led past Peter. He looked at him—straight at him. No words were needed, for God can use a common cockerel to speak more pungently than the human tongue. Peter realized he was captive still and that the road ahead was destined to be harder than the one he had so far traveled.

II

Why did he do it? One thing is sure; it is not that he had turned against Jesus and wanted him out of the way. Some will deny from hate or revenge. Not Peter. No one loved Jesus more than the man who so cruelly denied him. But this only underlines a strange trait in human behavior—those we love most, we hurt most. Love needs to be kept in good repair; the last thing we should do with love is to take it for granted.

He denied for his own selfish ends. He was scared. He denied because his nature was prone this way—to unreliability and quick temper.

Peter figures prominently in all four Gospels, where the image is of a man who committed blunder after blunder. He was disposed to "putting his foot in it"—an irritating though sometimes fascinating complaint! He is every inch a human being, but more lovable because of it!

His mistakes were many. But there is a revealing thing about them—*they come to us on his approval.* Mark's gospel, on which both Matthew and Luke draw a great deal, is to a large extent Peter's reminiscences, so in allowing these stories to be told against himself, he reveals a man of marvelous humility.

"The man who never made a mistake," said Robert Louis Stevenson, "never made anything." Of this Peter is a classic example, and his followers are many.

The young Winston Churchill is said to have made so many outrageous blunders that the press damned him for his "lack of discretion and judgment." Fortunately he did not allow this to undermine his confidence.

George Bernard Shaw said: "A man . . . progresses in all things by resolutely making a fool of himself."

No man is born into maturity—and this is a sobering thought! I am sure God plans it this way so that we need never get inflated with our own importance. We start life with the wonderful advantage of being potential blunderers! The first twenty years or so are spent in growing up—years that are littered with inevitable mistakes. Nor do they end there. They may lessen with maturity, but who will dare claim to have outgrown them?

We may be discouraged by them and give in to the despair of self-pity, or we may learn the lessons they teach and turn them to our good. This is what God's greatest servants always did. They made mistakes; they confessed to them, but were prepared to admit that even these might be within the wise providence of God. There was Abraham. One impetuous moment produced the illegitimate Ishmael—and no more serious blunder is made than when it jeopardizes a human life. But God says: "As for Ishmael, I will bless him." He takes care of our blunders and loves us in spite of them—never holding them against us. Without this, life would be unlivable.

Nowhere is this better illustrated than in the relationship between Jesus and Simon Peter.

Here is this "muscular fellow with a strong, impulsive vocabulary," forever making rash promises and asking naive questions. He blundered like a novice and queried like a schoolboy, *but Jesus never gave him up*. Who else would have put up with him?

From the evidence of the Gospels it would seem that Jesus made a big mistake in choosing Peter in the first place. By modern day procedure he would have "shopped around" a little more and considered a few testimonials.

But if the Gospels give this impression, the book of Acts and Peter's own letters tell another story, leaving us in no doubt that Jesus knew exactly what he was doing, and how right he was on that day beside the lake when he called the brawny fisherman to be his disciple. He knew Peter better than Peter knew himself.

This is always the way with Jesus. He sees possibilities in the most unlikely people—people who do not appear either to themselves or to others to possess any special talents. He would ignore the worst testimonial!

Sir Linton Andrews, the well-known journalist, writes of an editor who interviewed candidates for jobs. As they proudly presented their references and testimonials he would say, "Never mind what you did last year, or even yesterday. What can you do today and tomorrow and next year? It is your future work I have to assess."

Jesus was interested in Peter's potential, not his pedigree. There was a greatness about him which he knew would one day justify his choice. Francis James wrote: "Often I am haunted by the memory of what I have been, and often tortured by the knowledge of what I am. Yet there is something that I would be, something far different." This speaks of Peter too.

"You will be called 'Cephas'"—the Aramaic equivalent of the Greek *petros—rock*. This was his potential. Now he was still the impulsive, unreliable Simon, and there would be errors galore before he took on leadership of the young church. The shifting sands of his enthusiastic love must first solidify into the granite rock needed for the job.

At times he showed what he would be, not least on that memorable day on the road to Caesarea Philippi when he made the profound statement of faith in Christ as "Son of the Living God." Jesus appreciated that, and it became a turning point in his ministry. Yet only a little later the same impetuous Peter got a stern rebuke.

"Away with you Satan; you are a stumbling-block to me." There is a feeling of those early wilderness temptations about it. Peter meant well. He always did. All he had attempted was to divert Jesus from his proposal, which affronted Peter, to suffer death. Surely it hurt Jesus to reprimand him like this, but if Peter was to be shaped for the future there was no other way.

Of what use were those rash promises? "All of you will be offended at me," said Jesus. "Not me," exploded Peter; "I will give my life for you." It was one thing to promise, but another to practice. The intention was sincere, but like all noble intentions and good resolutions, they remain mere words unless put to the test. And the test came with shattering consequences.

The man who affirmed unbreakable loyalty to his Master was to experience the fulfillment of a dreadful warning—"I tell you, tonight before the cock crows you will disown me three times."

It is an all too human story that shows man's basic instinct to survive.

As Jesus was led from the garden of prayer, Peter followed behind, alone, and found himself in the courtyard of the high priest's house. As he sat huddled in his cloak by a charcoal fire, a servant girl suddenly recognized him as the flickering flames revealed his features.

"You too were with Jesus of Galilee," she said. He leaped in fear and blurted, "I don't know what you are talking about."

Then another girl accused him, but he was more prepared this time. "I swear that I don't know this man."

And sure enough came the third charge. "Of course you are one of them; after all, the way you speak gives you away." Peter's accent was Galilean, and the Aramaic of Galilee like the Aramaic spoken there today had dialectical peculiarities.

Peter was in it too deeply now. So in a last despairing attempt for freedom he made his thoughtless defense—as impetuous as anything he had ever done. "May God punish me," he said, "if I am not telling the truth."

And the cock crowed. It was the worst sound he had ever heard, and Peter, sick with remorse, burst into tears.

42

III

Denials come in a thousand ways. The deadliest are not written on paper or declared from platforms. Most are never spoken at all—they are lived.

The world's hungry and homeless cry in their misery for bread and board. Like it or not, we are "our brother's keeper." If we do nothing, we deny.

People are said to want the church for the occasions of "hatch, match, and despatch." Maybe. Public opinion polls indicate that few would wish the churches to close. Most parents are said to want religious instruction to remain in our day schools. Certainly the church is called upon to add an aura of respectability to most of our civic and social functions. In short—God is an asset if he doesn't ask too much. Paul must have had this sort of person in mind when he wrote, "they preserve the outward form of religion, but are a standing denial of its reality." On Sundays a minority know their need of God and make their way to church, but multitudes never bother. The temporal seems more attractive than the eternal—golf seems far better than God—and it appears not to make any difference.

But man has a destiny beyond his earthly life, for God has opened up eternity to the human race, and to disregard this is to deny our basic worth. It is to deny the greatness of such a gift and to spurn the love of the Giver.

Middleton Murray declared: "After Jesus lived and died in it, the world was never the same again." If this is so then the most serious offence we commit against him is not to be an opponent of his cause—

sad though that is. It is to ignore him—to pay no attention to his claims:

Just as if Jesus had never lived,
As if he had never died.

But denial is not practiced only by the irreligious or the indifferent. Believers also deny. Peter was a great believer and passionately committed. His own painful experience therefore poses an equally painful question for those of us who claim the name of Christ—*when did you last put yourself in a hot spot?*

"But," you say, "this is not for me. I know my limitations. I would lose my temper and say things I would regret. No, if people want to stand hard on religious principles, it's up to them, but I'm for keeping at a distance." Denial then is in silence as much as in words—in the refusal to "get involved." We are members of Christ's church. We professed our allegiance to him. We said that we would love and serve him always, and be his witnesses in the world. Are we now asking for a Christianity without crisis? A Christ without a cross? A fair-weather following?

This is blatant denial. It is to repudiate our Lord's basic command. We are to "deny ourselves and take up the cross." Indeed, he has warned us that if we have not the faith to live dangerously, we may well lose what we tried so hard to preserve. Faith is said to be like a pair of legs—it grows strong through exercise! Is it not then part of the Christian's exercise to be found also amongst that uneasy company in which we may be challenged to account for the faith we hold?

"Do not pray for easy lives," said Phillips Brooks, "pray to be stronger men. Do not pray for tasks equal to your powers, but for powers equal to your tasks." This we must do though our words falter and our defenses take a battering.

Peter denied. But to attempt something difficult and find it too hard is not to have failed. It is to have learned; to have taken exercise and be the stronger for it. In this way Peter is an example to us. He will never be forgotten as a headstrong vacillating man. His denial, like Judas's betrayal, is legend. Think of denial and you think of Peter. But to see his weaknesses alone is to misunderstand him for great strength of will was required to put himself in that position where failure was more dramatically possible.

That he was there at all is to give him credit. He denied his Lord, but so did all the other disciples. They were not there for safety's sake; Peter *was* there, though despairingly "to see the end," but he was there.

There is a saying: "Every cock crows on its own dunghill." In other words, it is easy to brag of your deeds in your own castle when safe from danger and not likely to be put to the proof! Peter would know what that meant.

We cannot talk of denials being better or worse. They have no virtue, except that some are born of courage. I know this much—should I choose to emulate any one of those disciples, it would be Peter. And if circumstances should force me to deny my Lord, I pray it may be as his—denial that comes from the courage of involvement rather than from the cowardice of absence.

I know too that I cannot condemn Peter. Jesus didn't. The Sioux Indians had a most apt prayer: "Great Spirit, help me never to judge another until I have walked for two miles in his moccasins."

"There but for the grace of God. . . ."

His crowing is the sound of vigilance. From its position on top of a steeple the weather-cock not only gives a clue to the weather; it is an old symbol of watchfulness. That today it is hidden by towering concrete blocks is to draw out a lesson of subtle significance.

The crowing cock is never far from us.

> *You cruel brute!*
> *You feathered fiend to mock me to my face!*
> *Do you not understand the human heart that*
>   *longs to beat securely*
> *And be at ease from fear?*
> *I hate you and the grating of your voice.*
> *You're right of course,*
> *As he was right,*
> *But did you have to do exactly as he said?*
> *—Yet I know I need to hear you,*
> *For now I really know;*
> *I must not hate what teaches me the truth.*
> *You are my warning,*
> *And when this mourning passes*
> *You my dawning*
> *Will spur me on to faithful service yet.*

The quick-tempered, otherwise alert Peter, had his relapses. Like the rest of them he was not able to keep awake when Jesus needed him most.

"Asleep, Simon? Were you not able to stay awake for one hour? Stay awake all of you; and pray that you may be spared the test."

46

I don't doubt that he has to caution us too for our lethargy, for we sometimes behave as if the work of the kingdom was complete from which we can now rest. But nothing is further from the truth. When we became members of the church of Jesus Christ we were not given a certificate of merit or told that we had arrived at our destination. Rather, we had set out on a pilgrimage. To go to sleep too near the place where we got in may be a good excuse for the little girl who fell out of bed, but in terms of Christian discipleship it is a tragedy.

"We thank thee that thy church unsleeping . . ."

I suspect this is more a prayer of what ought to be than of what is! For is it not characteristic of us to be alert to unimportant things and hypersensitive to trivialities, yet ignore the really crucial concerns of the kingdom? We are wide awake when self stands to lose but asleep when Christ may chance to gain.

Dr. W. E. Sangster underlines this danger: "It is hard to blame people for not being vigilant," he says, "but that is how wickedness wins its way in this world. It counts on the sleepiness and comfort-loving character of the good, and it wins."

> *Principalities and powers,*
> *Mustering their unseen array,*
> *Wait for thy unguarded hours:*
> *Watch and pray.*

The crowing cock would have us keep awake.

But one thing more. *He is the sound and symbol of a new beginning.*

The cock heralds the dawn. As the grey light of morning broke through into the courtyard, it spoke to Peter of the end and the beginning. It was the end of rash promises and boyish blunders, though not the end of taking risks—that was about to begin. Peter realized at last that he was too intimately related to Jesus ever to get away from him.

And those we love deeply we do not wish to give up. We believe in them in spite of themselves. And this is the way with Jesus. He judges, but always in love. He does not condemn; he renews. He sees us more by what we can become than by what we have been. He grants us the priceless chance to start again.

Peter begins his "new day" by dashing first to the tomb. The man who went to "see the end" is there to see the beginning.

"Give this message to his disciples—and Peter."

"And Peter." Then, following a fruitless night's fishing, he stands on the shore with his Master, just as he did three years before.

"Do you love me, Peter?" Three times he asked him—as if to cancel those three denials. "You know, Lord, that I love you."

"Feed my sheep."

Ransomed, healed, restored, forgiven . . .

Soon he is defending his Master with total disregard for his own safety. He is once more recognized as having "been with Jesus," only this time he is not crouching incognito in some dark corner. Now he is proud of it. He wants the world to know. He will indeed die rather than deny.

"The question we have to answer," says John Oman, "is, who has succeeded to Peter's power? The pope may indeed be a true successor of Peter, but the further the pope is from his infallibility and sovereignty, the truer successor he is to the impulsive, erring, but loyal-hearted apostle, and then, as God judges, the stronger he is as a rock on which to build a church."

O Lord Jesus Christ, look upon us with those eyes of thine wherewith thou didst look upon Peter in the hall; that with Peter we may repent, and, by the same love, be forgiven; for thine endless mercies' sake.

Bishop Andrewes (adapted)

4

THE CLATTER
of COINS

And Judas flung down the silver in the Temple and went away and hanged himself.

Matthew 27:5 Phillips

> *Thine own disciple to the Jews has*
> *sold thee;*
> *With friendship's kiss and loyal*
> *word he came:*
> *How oft of faithful love my lips have*
> *told thee,*
> *While thou hast seen my falsehood*
> *and my shame!*

I

"Beg that thou may'st have leave to hang thyself. . . ."

"Art thou contented Jew—what dost thou say?"

"I am content. I pray thee give me leave to go from hence."

Stubborn persistence is so often blind to snags. Shylock got more than he bargained for, though what he really wanted was beyond his means to pay.

So it was with Judas—though his intentions were different from those of the measly Merchant of Venice.

Still, he bears the despicable brand—*traitor*—a man who violates his allegiance. A traitor will sell his country or comrades to the enemy to line his own pocket or save his own skin. Country or comrades— is there a difference? E. M. Forster said: "If I had to choose between betraying my country and betraying my friend, I hope I should have the guts to betray my country."

If to betray a friend is that bad, small wonder Judas gets little sympathy!

Fatalists say he was predestined to be a traitor; pietists argue he was totally depraved; dramatists depict him as the incarnation of Satanic wickedness; whilst Dante characteristically sets him in the lowest depths of frozen Hell. No man can have had worse things said of him or been placed so utterly beyond redemption. Who indeed would name their child "Judas"?

Unfortunately, we are prone to judge a man more by his misdeeds than by his virtues. All men have goodness in them—Judas among them. After all, Jesus chose him to be one of his disciples, and all along seems well aware of his weaknesses, yet he never sacked him from the company, not even when he knew the monstrous plot the "betrayer" had in mind. Jesus in fact singled him out for a special job, appointing him treasurer of the group—a recognition, surely, that he could be trusted to handle money matters.

Judas never began as a traitor; he became one. The reasons are not easy to determine and all are open to question. We shall consider two issues which have a bearing on this dastardly act—*money* and *politics.*

II

It is widely held that **Judas betrayed for money.** Certainly money was involved—which is not surprising for a "keeper of the purse." He was gifted, as we have seen, but instead of using his gift he allowed his gift to use him and in the end to destroy him. Was he overfond of money? Maybe he had turned a deaf ear to what Jesus had said about this kind of thing making it hard for a man to enter the kingdom.

He was all for economy. There was that occasion when Mary of Bethany anointed Jesus with expensive ointment, and Judas was indignant at the waste: "Why was this perfume not sold for 300 denarii and given to the poor?"

It was a generous thought but John, who alone records it, remarks caustically that Judas cared nothing for the poor and that all he was interested in was the money—"he was a thief and stole from the purse." In fairness we should note that there is no reference in John's gospel to the synoptic tradition that Judas sold Jesus for money.

He certainly did love money. Whatever motivated his act of betrayal, he took money for it. The deal had to involve money. The most diabolical plans always do. To quote E. M. Forster in *Howards End*—"Give Mr. Bast money, and don't worry about his ideals."

"Money," says Gottfried Reinhardt, "is good for bribing yourself through the inconveniences of life."

What followed is only too well known. Caiaphas and his confederates had been on the lookout for someone who knew Jesus well and whom they could bluff and use; and they found him—one of the inner group who had been with the Galilean all along. It was unbelievable luck; they never even made the first approach—Judas just walked in.

"What will you give me to betray him to you?" he asked. In an instant they weighed him out 30 silver pieces. It was an opportunity not to be missed. The disciple whose frustration led to unscrupulous intrigue was to eat the bitter fruit of disobedience. He became a puppet in the hands of crafty operators, and what a degrading thing this always is! There they were "as thick as thieves," and poor Judas was either too excited or just not wise enough to see what was happening. They led him to believe that *he* was the prime mover and that a friendship bond had been forged between them. Little did he know that they wanted him for other reasons than merely identifying his master in a crowd. They had ideas beyond what he intended. We can only speculate on the sort of questions they might have asked him about Jesus—What had he told the Twelve about himself? What were his intentions? This was the most promising moment of Judas's life, but in his excitement, just how much "inside information" did he inadvertently proffer?

"Friendship" indeed! There is no honor among scoundrels. The cash agreement was the only thing that held them together, and when the deal was transacted Judas was of no more use.

It was a case then of each party attempting to hoodwink the other. Judas had ulterior motives, as we shall see, at the same time Jewish officialdom itself was hoping to inveigle Judas into "talking."

Poor Judas! It dawned on him now what was likely to happen, and it was too awful for words. Caiaphas had missed the point—deliberately! Judas had failed to persuade and to manipulate the high priest; instead he had sentenced his own leader to death.

"But I have betrayed innocent blood."

"What is that to us? See to that yourself."

He got his 30 shekels—something less than five pounds, but it meant nothing, as he demonstrated dramatically.

The sound effect of coins thrown in anger on a stone floor needs little description. Their embarrassing clatter echoes Judas's desolation. He had lost all. The hopes he once had in Jesus are now shattered, and those he thought were kindly disposed have abandoned him to his misery. It had all gone so terribly wrong. What he intended was to collect his "fiver," get away as fast as he could and await the desired outcome. As soon as his plans showed signs of materializing he would be back, ready to be his master's right-hand man.

But Jesus said of the man who was to betray him: "It would be better if he had never been born." What pathos lies in these words! When it dawned on Judas just what he had done he found it impossible to go on living. He discovered, albeit too late, what all in their disobedience have discovered, that no one can maltreat Jesus without severe consequences. He learned too what multitudes have learned since, that subtle dangers lie in a man's worldly skill, especially for one whose job it is to handle money; misuse this expertise and disaster is swift and sure.

Michel Quoist puts it well in his "Prayer before a Five Pound Note": "We can hardly respect money enough for the blood and toil it represents. Money is frightening. It can serve or destroy man."

Judas would agree.

III

"Money is the root of all evil" said a once-popular song. This is a misquote, as we know. Money in itself is a necessity and is meant for good use; evil lies rather in the "love" of money. It is not wrong to possess it, but it is wrong to love it and misuse it. How we are to stop the canker of competitive greed eating its way into the vitals of society is one of the great problems of our money-motivated age.

Mahatma Ghandi once said to a group of his fellow Indians: "You will understand your Western friends much better if you remember that no matter what they say in creed or in church, money is their real god."

And it *is* a god for many. There are modern day Scrooges who take simple pleasure in hoarding their money. They are misers. Money must beget money so they make regular offerings to the god of investment. To hoard it, overlove it, and worship it is quite wrong.

It is equally wrong to believe money can get just anything, for are there not many things "without money and without price"? But this was Judas's fatal mistake. He was one who could price any commodity—understandable as far as commodities are concerned, but a serious aptitude when it comes to *"pricing people."* The slave markets of the ancient world, and indeed of more recent history, were mercifully abolished, though they may be seen to exist in the more sophisticated realm of professional sport and big business where a man of talent is assessed as a likely money-spinner!

But who can estimate the worth of any man? Jesus made friends—even disciples of men whom others had written off. He restored the dignity of outcasts and sinners; he said that not even a common sparrow falls to the ground without God knowing, so how much is he aware of what happens to human beings who are of infinitely greater value? Why, even the very hairs of a man's head are all numbered! Only a fool then would attempt to estimate in cash terms what a man is worth.

And only a bigger fool would price Jesus himself. Thirty shekels was said to be the customary price of a slave in those days, and Judas settled for that in exchange for his master—which shows the blinding, dehumanizing effect of money. But it was a futile attempt from the start, for if Judas had offered the wealth of the world, it would have made no difference, for Jesus is beyond price.

The point is put brilliantly by Joseph Beaumont, a seventeenth century poet:

> *But thou, improvident Judas, since thou art*
> *Resolved to sell a thing whose value is*
> *Beyond the power of arithmetic art*
> *To reckon up—proportionate thy price*
> *In some more near degree; let thy demand*
> *   Make buyers, who this Christ is, understand.*
>
> *Ask all the gold that rolls on Indus' shore,*
> *Ask all the treasures of the eastern sea,*

Ask all the earth's yet undiscovered ore,
Ask all the gems and pearls which purest be,
 Ask Herod's' chequer, ask the high priest's crown,
 Ask Caesar's mighty sceptre and his throne.

Ask all the silver of the glistening stars,
Ask all the gold that flames in Phoebus' eyes,
Ask all the jewels of Aurora's tears,
Ask all the smiles and beauties of the skies,
 Ask all that can by anything be given,
 Ask bliss, ask life, ask paradise, ask heaven.

Someone else movingly describes how invaluable is the life of Christ: "He possessed neither wealth nor influence; his relatives were inconspicuous and had neither training nor formal education. In infancy he startled a king; in childhood he puzzled doctors of the Law. In manhood he ruled the course of nature, walked upon the billows as if pavements, and hushed the sea to sleep. He healed the multitudes without medicine and made no charge for his services. He never wrote a book, yet not one library could hold all the books that have been written about him. He never wrote a song, yet he has furnished the theme for more songs than all the song writers combined. He never founded a college, but all the schools put together cannot boast of having as many students. He never marshaled an army nor drafted a soldier nor fired a gun, and yet no leader ever had more volunteers. He was never trained in psychiatry and yet he has healed more broken hearts than all psychiatrists put together. Each week multitudes wend their way to pay homage to him and to receive knowledge of him. The names of past proud statesmen have come and gone, but his name abounds more and more. Over nineteen hundred years have passed since he lived on earth—

yet he still lives. The grave could not hold him. Adored by saints and feared by devils—we are either going to be forever with him or forever without him."

It is unbelievable that such a life should once have been reduced in human estimation to a commercial equivalent in cash; that he who is beyond price should be priced as a slave. And yet our Lord's purpose is fulfilled in this very spectacle of humiliation, for he "made himself nothing, assuming the nature of a slave" in order to redeem sinful humanity.

Judas may be partly excused for not knowing what Jesus would become; he acted on the little that he knew then, yet it surely was enough to make him wise and check him from betrayal. But a man incensed with the belief that money can get anything is likely to stop at nothing.

> Urge him no more with sense and reason; he
> Resolves to traffic with the priests; for now
> No other god but money he can see—
> He nothing sees at all, and cares not how
> He makes his bargain with them so he may
> Have but this wretched sum in ready pay.

IV

But money, important as it was in this affair, was but the means to a much greater end. Judas showed this when he threw down the 30 shekels. **The principal motive, surely, was political.**

Why is Judas "the solitary Southerner in a bunch of Northerners?" What was he doing in Galilee? Was he already known to the Romans as a political agitator? Did not Judas believe that Jesus could fulfill his political dreams?

It was exciting to follow the Galilean; his words were revolutionary; he was daring enough to knock time-honored traditions and assert his own authority—"It has been said by those of old time, but I say to you." He brushed aside scribal food restrictions and Levitical taboos. Here were obvious qualities that impressed Judas and which he thought he might exploit. Nor was it all talk. He did things which proved he possessed unusual powers, which all seemed necessary for the enterprise Judas had in mind.

But hopes were soon dashed—and pointlessly it seemed. Following the miraculous feeding some 5000 people would have made him king on the spot, but he refused. This was a bitter disappointment and Judas was baffled, and it is from the moment of that inexplicable decision that relationships begin to deteriorate. Jesus loses his crowd appeal, and the ever-watchful Pharisees begin planning his arrest in earnest. All the disciples are bewildered.

And what danger lurks in a moment of reaction! Judas's patience runs out, and Jesus, we are told, sees in him the germ of a traitor spirit—"he knew who was to betray him." Hopes soared again as Jesus entered Jerusalem to thunderous acclaim, but when he made it quite clear he was not intending to be the leader of a revolt against Rome, at that point Judas's dream was crushed. Certainly, Jesus spoke of a kingdom over which he would be king, but it was far from what his frustrated disciple had in mind.

But Judas was a determined man. Maybe all was not lost. He was sure of one thing—his patience had gone unrewarded, and the time for waiting was over; he just had to force the issue.

He knew that a trapped animal will fight for its life—so if Jesus is put to the extreme test and cornered would he not unleash those strange powers in his own defense? Surely he would at last see the lethargy of his fellow countrymen who had been lulled to sleep by Rome, and would he not surrender his previous notions of peace by peaceful means?

There was only one way to find out—*create the situation*. He would negotiate with the top brass of Jewish officialdom—he had no time left to do otherwise. Caiaphas would doubtless be delighted to do business with a colleague of the upstart "Messiah" who had caused so much trouble. This would really stir up the right sort of trouble.

V

Judas should have known better. Had his master not refused many times to be drawn into political conflict? He should have learned by now *the futility of attempting to manipulate Jesus—of getting Jesus to be what he had no intention of being*. This was Judas's real sin.

And it is a common one. The Christian cause was still in its infancy when Paul was compelled to ask "Is Christ divided?" All too soon desire became the father of doctrine and Christ's image was twisted; he was a mere human or not human at all—hence the proliferation of credal statements to counteract heresy. But the distortions continued. Centuries of religious art, hymnology and, above all—behavior, testifies to the lopsidedness of human thinking about the person of Christ. Grotesque pictures have served only to mar his image. In his book on the life of Martin Luther, Roland Bainton includes a sketch typical of the times—Christ the fearsome judge is sitting upon a rainbow; from his left ear protrudes a sword, symbolizing the doom of the damned, whom the devils drag by the hair from the tombs and cast into the flames of hell!

Many times would Jesus fail to recognize himself! But it suited the church to represent him this way; so has it suited the church to imprison him in sectarian edifices, in wordy creeds, in special language. His name has sponsored a thousand causes—imperialism, anarchism, fascism, and others. His cross has been emblazoned on battle flags, and Christians never doubted the side he was on in their slaughterous crusades. Carlyle equated greatness in terms of heroes, so he made Jesus his favorite hero. Voltaire thought Jesus to be the greatest humanitarian of all time, while Renan's life of Christ is said to be "patently three parts Renan and one part Jesus."

But he will be a rubber-stamp for no man. He will toe the line of no cause, political or otherwise. He will give exclusive support to no sect. At the outset of his ministry he was tempted to take an alternative course to that for which he had been sent, and in refusing he made his intentions clear to all—he is subject to no man. The kingdoms of this world are his, and he has a way of his own which he relentlessly pursues against constant requests to deviate.

However devotedly we express our relationship to him, we are to remember that he does not belong to any one of us—indeed, too many distortions have followed the "Jesus is mine" theology popular in certain types of Christianity.

It was the mistake that Judas made; he just did not have the faith to take Jesus as he was. No, he never "sold" Jesus, for he never had him to sell; *he tried to buy him,* to get him to acquiesce in his own political aspirations, but Jesus, though cornered and condemned, would not yield.

Offer what you will, you can neither buy him nor employ him. You go his way or you do not go at all. No man can own him, but all men are subject to him:

> *He justly claims us for his own,*
> *Who bought us with a price;*
> *The Christian lives to Christ alone,*
> *To Christ alone he dies.*

Judas Iscariot found the cash not worth taking nor his life worth living, yet had he sought forgiveness of his master whom he shamefully betrayed, I believe he would have found it.

It is a tragic story with an ever poignant reminder.

Lord Jesus, you are who you are. No one can change you nor coerce you, and in this is our only hope. Lord, we follow you just as you are.

5

THE SPLASH of WATER

When Pilate saw that he wasn't getting anywhere, and that a riot was developing, he sent for a bowl of water and washed his hands before the crowd, saying, "I am innocent of the blood of this good man. The responsibility is yours!" Matthew 27:24 The Living Bible

> *Bearing shame and scoffing rude,*
> *In my place condemned he stood;*
> *Sealed my pardon with his blood:*
> *Hallelujah! What a Savior!*

I

Rita Snowden recalls one of her visits to Switzerland: "I raised my eyes above Lake Lucerne, to the misty heights of Mount Pilatus—named for him; and I listened to the legend that there on moonlit nights, the unquiet spirit of Pilate hovers above the waters of the lake, *forever washing his hands.*"

"Responsibility," she adds, "is not really to be got rid of that way."

We would agree. But I wonder what you or I would do under the same circumstances!

It seems only fair that if we are to appreciate the implications of Pilate's hand washing, we should try to understand the circumstances surrounding the man whose name is indelibly written across the centuries, and whom generations have looked on with contempt.

"Suffered under Pontius Pilate," says the church in "The Apostles' Creed." Granted, this serves as a useful date-mark, but just how fair is it? After all, there were others who caused Jesus far more suffering than did Pilate. In fact it was Pilate who, in another way, suffered under Jesus. Nonetheless history brands him, and the passing years have failed to erase the name of the Roman governor who washed his hands of Jesus.

Pontius Pilate was a man with problems. Indeed, his problems were so great that when on the one all-important occasion that he tried to do what he considered right and just, he found it was quite impossible. He was forced therefore to compromise, and of that compromise, the Creed is testimony.

He was sent to govern the hot-bed of Judea—a province of intense anti-Roman feeling. As it turned out, he was not the strongest man for the job. He realized, no doubt, that it was a tough assignment, but hardly could he have visualized problems so immense and insoluble.

It could be said he never stood a chance. Maybe not. Yet one has the impression he might have succeeded, partially at least, if he had curbed his anti-Semitism. He was prejudiced, and a prejudiced man is doomed from the start.

There was blunder number one. His predecessors, in their wisdom, had seen to it that Roman soldiers removed the images from their standards as they entered Jerusalem. They knew that such symbols were offensive to the Jews as idolatrous and could cause real trouble; it was better to keep the peace—always a good Roman policy. But Pilate did not follow suit, until persistent threats from a Jewish deputation forced him to give the order.

Blunder number two soon followed. On the walls of his palace residence in Jerusalem Pilate had fixed golden shields which bore the name of the Emperor. This was a clear case of Caesar worship, but once more Jewish persistence prevailed; this time the Jews went to the top—to Tiberius, and the emperor himself ordered Pilate to remove them.

A third careless blunder completed the rift between them. Jerusalem was short of water. When pilgrims crowded the city for festivals, the shortage was most acute. Pilate, with good intentions, took steps to improve the matter by building an aqueduct; this was fine, except that he financed it from the Temple funds! Not even the Jews could deny the need for such a project, and doubtless would have contributed to it, but Pontius Pilate had done it over their heads, and this was more than they could stand. Pandemonium broke out and blood was spilled.

It was clear now that the governor of Judea had had it! Any hope of success for him in this part of the world was now doomed. He made other mistakes later, and was finally ordered back to Rome, but this is unimportant in the present context.

What does matter for us is that during his governorship, a man, a Jew, was brought before him by

Jews, to be condemned to death. This was unfortunate for Pilate. Having made a mess of things already, he needed to retreat for a while from the forefront and let the inflamed situation cool—and it might have done so. Indeed, Pilate might have been inconspicuously remembered in the annals of Rome as another one of those procurators who did not achieve much success—*but that his office covered the period of the ministry of Jesus of Nazareth.*

II

This is to speak a profound truth about Jesus, for no man can face him as Pilate did without finding it to be the most crucial encounter of his life. For that reason I say it was Pilate who suffered under Jesus. A Jewish prisoner could hardly expect lenient treatment from this governor whose hatred for Jews was by this time as intense as their hatred for him, so we might expect that he would dismiss the accused for execution with casual and pleasurable contempt.

The prisoner was in fact condemned, as we know, *but only after Pilate had resisted his accusers by every possible means,* and this is to give credit to him which generations of Christians have failed to do. He wanted to release Jesus, and it is interesting to see how desperately hard he tried to do this. The Jewish Sanhedrin had no power to condemn a man to death, so they sent Jesus to Pilate, expecting him to pass sentence on their simple accusation that he was a criminal.

But Roman governors were trained lawyers—hence Pilate's refusal to sentence Jesus whom he believed to be innocent. Like any good lawyer, he took steps to examine the accusation in more detail. Upon investigation he discovered that this man's "criminal" deeds had been: "subverting the nation, opposing the payment of taxes to Caesar, and claiming to be 'Messiah,' a king."

Pilate thought these to be insufficient grounds for sentence of death—in fact, he seemed quite impressed about this "kingship" idea of the accused; at any rate he could see nothing subversive in it. Convinced then that Jesus had done nothing to deserve death, Pilate sought every means within his power to acquit him— if he could do it without again arousing the anger of the Jews. But he sought in vain.

Finding that Jesus came from Galilee, Pilate sent the prisoner to Herod Antipas who happened to be in Jerusalem for the feast. Herod was delighted. He had long wanted the chance of meeting the Galilean and seeing him perform a miracle. But Jesus did not oblige, neither by word nor deed, and in bitter disappointment Herod sent him back to Pilate.

This, thought Pilate, was an opportune time to propose acquittal. It was the governor's custom at the festival to release a prisoner of some notoriety; but the priests had been at work on the mob before the choice was put, so that Jesus was condemned while the murderer and revolutionary, Bar-Abbas, was discharged.

Pilate was desperate. He had known all along that the charge was false; given half a chance they would all have committed treason against Rome themselves. Anyway, had not the prisoner been brought to him out of spite because he had challenged them where it really hurt? To add to his many fears, his wife was now having nightmares about this Jesus.

Defeat stared him in the face, but he would make one final plea to human pity in the hope that they would spare the cross if not the whip. But he found none. Their verdict was merciless and final—"Crucify him!"

Pilate then "sent for a bowl of water and washed his hands. . . . I am innocent of the blood of this good man. The responsibility is yours!"

So we remember him as the man who, in that act, shrugged off his responsibility for the death of Jesus. But the stain of innocent blood is not so easily removed.

We have to admit that under the extenuating circumstances, Pilate did what most others would have done. Faced as he was with the terrible choice of one man or many, there seemed little else he could do. A bloodbath would have followed had Jesus been released. Caiaphas the high priest had earlier said that he thought it was in the interests of the Jews that one man should die for the people rather than the nation itself be destroyed. Pilate's garrisons were too undermanned to cope with a riot, and his own background too disastrous to permit a further mistake. So he had really little choice. It might have been of some consolation that this one death would soon be forgotten, whereas a mass riot causing many deaths would be irreparable. Little did he know!

III

Pontius Pilate is history's classic buck passer. We have studied his circumstances, yet making every allowance possible, and absolving him as much as we can—he remains so.

"I am innocent . . . the responsibility is yours." But who can ever say this with complete confidence? Certainly not Pilate. He was very largely to blame for his own predicament, and his unpopularity with the Jews removed even the slightest possibility of Jesus' acquittal.

He has his followers in every age, for buck-passing is ancient and modern. The "scapegoat" upon which a man's sins were "transferred" has always been something of a psychological necessity, and, doubtless, of therapeutic value. But what a fiendish practice it can be!

Jesus was nailed to the cross by Roman soldiers, but they were not the real executioners; it was the Jews who were responsible—spiritually, morally, and emotionally, but of course, they passed the buck. "We have no king but Caesar," they declared, with characteristic hypocrisy. It was clear they would get anyone—even their most inveterate enemy—to do for them what their own religion forbade.

Roscini's brilliant "Twentieth Century Pieta" is a life-size sculpture depicting the removal of our Lord's body from the cross by a Roman soldier. Mary the mother of Jesus kneels beside her dead son with a look of stunned sorrow. But the really poignant feature of this work is the young soldier who, in emotional reaction, points an accusing finger at the crowd—at the onlooker, at society, at you and me—as if saying, "*You* did it." The idea came to the sculptor after watching a television documentary on the Vietnam war. A United States soldier, involved in the "Pinkville Massacre" defended his actions by saying: "It wasn't my fault; I was under orders."

In the business of military buck-passing, responsibility must rest somewhere.

Dr. Walter Rauschenbusch writes of Pilate's wash bowl. "On the eve of the crucifixion the wash bowl disappeared from the palace. Nobody knows who took it. At any rate, ever since that time, the wash bowl is abroad in the land, carried by infernal hands whenever it is needed, and men are constantly performing imperceptible ablutions therein. The statesman who suppresses principles because they might endanger the success of his party; the good citizen who will have nothing to do with politics; the editor who sees a righteous cause misrepresented, and says nothing; the preacher who sees Dives exploiting Lazarus and dares not tell him to quit, because Dives contributes to his salary; the Sunday school superintendent who sees a devoted teacher punctured by pinpricks of well-bred jealousy, and dares not champion her; all these are using Pilate's wash bowl. 'Listen!' he says, 'do you hear the splash of water near to you?'"

To be sure, the splash of water is heard in many a place. We have seen in the Northern Ireland conflict how prevalent it is for one side, Catholic or Protestant, to blame the other for some atrocity. In the ever present "war" between communist and noncommunist countries, each in turn resorts to some act of provocation—a prod here and there to try each other out, and when the situation flares up, as we have seen it do, one side will be sure to say—"They did it."

British politics were once the envy of the world, but the practice of buck-passing is, I believe, bringing it into disrepute. The government blames the opposition—"We inherited these problems from them,"

and the opposition declares how much more suc-
cessfully the country would be run if *they* and not the
others were in office—"it's the government's fault!"

The worker blames problems in his employment
on "the management," and may never consider the
part *he* may have played by dishonesty, laziness, and
greed.

And too often do we come across bureaucratic
buck-passing; failure to "deliver the goods," to get a
job done, is blamed on "shortage of staff" or on the
temperamental computer, or on the proverbial "they"
in head office, or wherever, who dragged their feet.
These are sometimes legitimate reasons, I don't
doubt, yet more and more I want to question the al-
leged innocence of those who too often and too easily
shift the blame.

Nor is it absent from the church. Though ecu-
menical relations are improving steadily, we are still
prone to blame "them"—some other denomination—
for lack of progress, or whatever the problem may be.
It is so easy, too, for the church to regard its declining
membership and diminishing influence as due to "social changes." Of course these changes have made a
difference, but the church cannot avoid taking a large
part of the blame upon itself. What of the unbelievable
complacency of the church during this very century
when social changes appeared inevitable, in which
the church failed considerably, and is still failing, to
adapt its ministry?

The church may criticize the "outsider" for not
wanting to attend, while ignoring the painful truth
that inside the church the presentation of so great a
gospel is but a pathetic caricature. Equally so will the
"outsider" lay excuse for his nonattendance on the

poor image of parsons, boring sermons, irrelevant hymns and all "those hypocrites who go."

In our own church or some local organization we easily shrug off some task that needs doing with the excuse that "so-and-so would do it much better." All this talk about "if you want a job done, give it to a busy person" is symptomatic of the same complaint.

Henry Ward Beecher reminds us that shifting responsibility is even possible in a service of worship. "The churches of the land," he says, "are sprinkled all over with bald-headed old sinners whose hair has been worn off by the constant friction of countless sermons that have been aimed at them and glanced off and hit the man in the pew behind. When we hear God's truth it is our duty to apply it not to other people, but to ourselves."

IV

"The fault dear Brutus, lies not in our stars but in ourselves." Such is the philosophy of the great ones of history and of all good leaders.

There was General Eisenhower, D-Day had already been postponed as a result of bad weather. When the chiefs met to reconsider the matter, the weather was still uncertain. With the fate of Europe in the balance "Ike" said, "I must take the decision; after all, that is what I am here for—we sail tomorrow." And when President Harry Truman succeeded to office, he place on his desk at the White House a card bearing a reminder of his lonely responsibility; on it was written, "the buck stops here."

It takes courage to say that and even greater courage to practice it. It certainly means headaches and heartaches. It could mean loss of prestige and popularity and the end of hopes for promotion. It might mean dismissal and even death. But nothing less is expected of a committed Christian.

"Every man," says Paul to the Galatians, "must shoulder his own pack" (J. B. Phillips's translation). We are not to go moaning about unfair disadvantages, or the odds against us, and making these alibis for our failures. Daniel Webster said that the greatest thought that ever came to him was that of his own personal responsibility to God. And he is right. Before God and man, the buck rests fairly and squarely on our own shoulders.

The prodigal son for all his faults was at least honest. He did not blame his father for being too lenient, nor his friends for leaving him when his money ran out, nor his employer for ill-treating him. He said: "I have sinned."

Pontius Pilate never did have the courage to say that. He knew Jesus was innocent, that the charge against him was nonsense, but he was weak-willed and afraid.

"If you let this man go you are not Caesar's friend," was the veiled threat that broke his resistance. It was not Jewish prejudice alone that had placed him in this awful situation, but also his own stubborn foolishness. In the end he had too much to lose.

"You take him then," he said to the Jews. And they did. "His blood be on us and on our children," they replied. They were to learn the bitter consequences of those words.

So Pilate handed him over and washed his hands of the whole sordid affair—or so he tried. But he has never gotten away with it, for we constantly remember that Jesus "suffered under Pontius Pilate, and was crucified. . . ."

But just in case we should think of shifting the blame on to him or on to the Jews or the Romans or on to anybody else, shall we not remember that it is the sort of sins we commit that involves us in our Savior's death:

> *Who was the guilty? Who brought this upon thee?*
> *Alas, my treason, Jesus, hath undone thee.*
> *'Twas I, Lord Jesus, I it was denied thee:*
> *I crucified thee.*

Pilate washed his hands, but he was involved once more—pressurized this time to change the inscription to read that Jesus "said" he was king of the Jews.

His reply is a classic; it encourages the heart and renews our hope in human beings: "What I have written, I have written."

That was one buck he did keep.

Lord Jesus, I think of the man who released you to your death. I think of the mess he had made of his life, and how he became trapped in his own foolishness. I think of how he feared for his own safety—and the more I think, the more I see Pontius Pilate in me. Lord forgive me. Help me to take my stand for you proudly, and without excuse.

6

THE THUD
of the HAMMER

Then they fastened him to the cross.   Mark 15:24

> *His feet and hands outstretching there,*
> *He willed the piercing nails to bear,*
> *For us and our redemption's sake*
> *A victim of himself to make.*
>
> *There whilst he hung, his sacred side*
> *By soldier's spear was opened wide*
> *To cleanse us in the precious flood*
> *Of water mingled with his blood.*

I

In *The Man Born to Be King* Dorothy L. Sayers puts words into the mouths of our Lord's executioners. The fourth soldier offers Jesus a drug to deaden the pain of the nails tearing into his flesh:

"Here, my lad—don't be obstinate. Drink it. It'll

deaden you like. You won't feel so much . . . No? . . .
Come on, then, get down to it."

The first soldier is less humane:

"Stretch your legs. I'll give you king of the Jews."

"Hand me the mallet."

"Father, forgive them. They don't know what
they are doing."

—His voice breaks off in a sharp gasp as the mallet falls, and fades out on the dull thud of the ham-
mering.

The events of Holy Week which culminated in
Jesus' crucifixion are nowhere more magnificently
dramatized than at Oberammergau in Bavaria every
10th year. This famous passion play has all the emotions, all the pictures, all the sounds—the crowds
shouting, jeering, weeping, the soldiers marching—
but there is no hammer blow, for the hands and feet
of the actor are bound rather than nailed to the cross.

No drama indeed can quite reenact that part of
Calvary.

It was Anton Lang who played the part of Christ
at Oberammergau just before the outbreak of the First
World War. He was a carpenter by trade. When war
came he was made to join the German army, but it
turned out that he was taken prisoner and brought
to England. On learning that he was a carpenter it
was decided not to put him among others in the pris-
oner-of-war camp, since he might be too handy with
tools, so they gave him a small hut to himself.

As Christmas drew near he thought of his wife
and two little children back home, and wished he
could make some Christmas presents for them. Then
he came upon three rusty nails and two small pieces

of wood. He polished and sharpened the nails until he had turned them into useful little chisels. One piece of wood he delicately carved into a cross, which he intended as a present for his wife, and the other piece he divided and made into two table serviette-rings. In spite of difficulties at first, for he was not supposed to have access to tools, he was allowed to send his presents home via the Red Cross.

It was with wood and nails that the carpenter from Nazareth expressed the overwhelming love in his heart for all humanity. The wooden cross to which he was nailed is a unique emblem, it stretches across the centuries telling of a love that went to the limits of suffering and self-giving—for "God so loved the world that he gave his only Son." It is Christianity's universal symbol; before it men rise in adoration and bow in contrition.

No wood was ever put to more shameful use nor more gloriously transformed than that which held his body.

II

As a carpenter, Jesus was well used to the sound of the hammer striking a nail. It is a sobering fact and worthy of recall, that before Jesus began his ministry of preaching, teaching, and healing, he had been practicing his faith at a workman's bench. We may be sure that what he produced in that long period of training was of the highest quality:

> *The yokes he made were true,*
> *Because the man who dreamed*
> *Was too*
> *An artisan,*

The burdens that the oxen drew
Were light.
At night
No beast of his stood chaffing
*   in a stall,*
Made restless by a needless gall.

"Come to me," he said "all whose work is hard, whose load is heavy, and I will give you relief . . . my yoke is good to bear, my load is light." But for himself—a heavy yoke, a rough-hewn cross.

The terrible spectacle of crucifixion would hardly be unfamiliar to Jesus. When he was a boy in Nazareth the Jews broke out in revolt barely five miles away, and Josephus, the historian, referring to this says that Romans crucified 2000 revolutionaries along the wayside.

The cross was Rome's ultimate deterrent, conveniently placed on the busy highways as a warning to all would-be rioters: "Thus are the enemies of Caesar treated."

Some years ago Israeli archaeologists discovered in a hillside cave near Jerusalem the first ever remains of a crucified victim from the time of Jesus. Though the bones had deteriorated they were able to draw a rough sketch. He was a young, lithe man, and the marks in the bones show that the nails were hammered into the forearms between the ulner and radial bones, and not in the palms. Nails in the palms would be insufficient to carry the weight of the body, and would tear them through. The legs of this particular victim were twisted up and a seven inch nail driven through the heel bones.

"Far be the cross from the eyes and ears of a

Roman citizen," said Cicero. It was meant to strike fear into the hearts of all people, and doubtless it did. Law-abiding folk would take one surreptitious glance, shudder with a cold feeling of insecurity, and walk quickly by.

No wonder Jesus prayed, "Father, save me from this hour."

For this was the worst form of torture and death ever devised, and any method was preferable to it. In one of his dialect poems, Studdert Kennedy has a soldier saying that he would "back them rusty nails agin a shell." So unparalleled is the cross in the torment it produced.

But for a Jew, crucifixion carried the additional spiritual torture of being thought abandoned by God: "Cursed is everyone who hangs on a tree," says the Law, and something of this is felt in our Lord's pitiful cry, "My God, my God, why have you forsaken me?"

"The cross," as someone has said, "was hard wood, hard nails, hard fact, hard lines." And the carpenter from Nazareth knew all about it.

I suggest that in the two instruments of crucifixion, hammer and nail, we find a most significant meaning. They symbolize *finality* and *unity*. The idea is conveyed in some words of Jeremiah the prophet when he is denouncing man-made idols: "A tree from the forest is cut down and worked with an axe by the hands of a craftsman. Men deck it with silver and gold; they fasten it with hammer and nails so that it cannot move."

III

A hammer is the symbol of finality. It clinches transactions. An auctioneer's hammer strikes and the commodity bid for is sold. A written contract is officially stamped and the deal is complete. A trigger releases its gun-hammer, the shot is irretrievably fired—perhaps ending some human life. Says James Stephens: "Finality is death."

Jesus might have avoided the decisive hammer by recanting at the eleventh hour. The temptation not to go through with it is hinted at in his agony in the garden. This is not to be thought a revelation of weakness of will, but rather of how truly human he was.

After all, who wants to die at 33? Certainly not Jesus. He loved life. He enjoyed the inexhaustible splendor of God's handiwork in nature. He saw God's great care in birds of the air and flowers of the field. He heard God speak in a man's daily work and a woman's family chores, indeed, every minute of the day produced opportunities to demonstrate his Father's love, and he wanted so much to go on grasping these opportunities. Life could never be long enough for his great purpose.

Before his death at the age of 49, Cecil Rhodes of South Africa sighed: "So little done, so much to do." And was it not so for Jesus?

The problem of "willing martyrs" arose quite soon in the early Christian church. Christians, believing that the world order would very soon end, courted martyrdom, convinced that such a pious sacrifice of their lives would bring immediate spiritual rewards. Paul and others had great difficulty in quelling such misguided enthusiasm, and rightly so. No man is expected to surrender his life cheaply, and to do so is surely to insult the divine giver. We must rather live it to the full, and only in the most extreme need, and for the very highest motive, should we dare surrender it.

That he asked for the bitter cup to pass him by is not merely to see our Lord's dread of the cross. It is to see even more his appreciation of life.

But here is the great paradox. Loving life, he yet chose death. Nor was it a last-minute, impetuous choice. It was one he made at the outset of his compassionate ministry in choosing to love as he did. Love has its extremity which is a willingness to prove our love by dying for those we profess to love—as Jesus put it: "There is no greater love than this that a man should lay down his life for his friends." He had committed himself to carrying love to its extremity, and it is on the cross where the hammer struck the final outreach of his love that we see the whole purpose of Christ. Toyohiko Kagawa, that great Japanese Christian, puts it well:

> As in a single word, Christ's love-movement
> Is summed up in the Cross. The Cross is
> The whole of Christ, the whole of love.
> God speaks to man through the Cross
> Of love's mysteries concealed in the divine bosom.

There is a finality in the cross of Christ, for beyond it God's love just cannot go, and it is this that makes Calvary unique. There were crucifixions before and after, but not one was like this. So unmatched was this one event that every generation since has looked to it as the final and all-perfect sacrifice. Though the sacrament of bread and wine in some church traditions speaks of Christ offering himself again, this can never be more than metaphorical, for there can be no repetition of Calvary.

Paul preached this with certainty; what the Law could not do, Jesus did, "having canceled the bond which stood against us with its legal demands, this he set aside, nailing it to the cross." Similarly, the author of the letter to the Hebrews, in contrasting the old and the new orders, states this point clearly: "The Jewish High Priest goes into the Holy Place every year with the blood of an animal. But Christ did not go in to offer himself many times; for then he would have had to suffer many times ever since the creation of the world. Instead, he has now appeared *once and for all*, when all ages of time are nearing the end to remove sin through the sacrifice of himself. Everyone must die once, and after that be judged by God. In the same manner, Christ also was offered in sacrifice *once* to take away the sins of many."

Jesus heard the hammer strike once more as Pontius Pilate nailed his inscription to the wood above him. It read: "Jesus of Nazareth, king of the Jews." It was written in Hebrew, Latin, and Greek. There was a storm of protest from the Jewish authorities who wanted it altered to read: "He claimed to be king of the Jews." But the hammer had struck and the verdict remained—"What I have written, I have written."

In every way the cross is God's consummating act of love, unrepeatable and unalterable.

Nor is there any substitute for it. Hebrew, Latin, and Greek—all three traditions had their substitute remedies for man's sin.

The Jews found a solution in the annual substitutionary sacrifice made by the high priest in the Temple, by which the people's sins were expiated or "atoned" for. This, together with a sound knowledge of the Torah would be sufficient. The Roman answer lay in law and order. The Emperor's decrees and the Senate's legislation made sure that citizens of the empire "toe the line." The Greek turned to art and enlightenment. In the beauty of nature and art he found aesthetic fulfillment, and in the wisdom of the philosopher—"the stimulus of the mental hike"—he found intellectual satisfaction.

All three convictions have their parallels in our present society. Some may be helpful but they are no more than substitute solutions to man's radical dilemma. *Man is a sinner in need of salvation, and he cannot save himself.* He is answerable for every sin he commits. He can know the law and still be lawless. He is not made worthy by act of parliament nor made good by human ingenuity. Before the cross of Jesus these classic substitutes are rendered obsolete:

> *All for sin could not atone;*
> *Thou must save, and thou alone.*

IV

And a nail is the symbol of unity. It joins together what is separate.

It was of course the cross-beam only and not the pillar that Jesus carried through the streets of Jerusalem. The failure of his strength along the way, which led to Simon of Cyrene carrying it for him, was probably due not so much to the weight of the load but the physical exhaustion caused by scourging.

Before his body was fastened to the wood Jesus would have heard the sound of the hammer striking a nail as the cross-beam was joined to the upright stanchion. The symbol is then complete, for the cross is two-dimensional—perpendicular and horizontal. When Jesus hung there on that framework with taut body and outstretched arms, he symbolized for ever a religion that is both upward and outward.

His own life was a brilliant demonstration of this. When asked which is the first commandment he replied: "Thou shalt love the Lord thy God." And what love he had for his Father, and what hours he must have spent in quiet communion with him! Indeed, we may be sure that before any day was spent in "going about doing good" he first "departed into a solitary place."

This is an obligation we ignore at great cost. We launch our social reforms and good causes and often forget that "the touchstone of ethics is the kingdom of God"—a kingdom which is also "not of this world." We need to pray as much as we need to eat. As the Psalmist put it: "Except the Lord build the house, they labor in vain that build it." Jesus' life was vertical in prayer and praise.

At the same time it was horizontal towards all men. "The second commandment" he said, "is this: Thou shalt love thy neighbor." In this way he gave the Ten Commandments their right interpretation and linked the old covenant with the new gospel. The geometry of the gospel is really set at his birth where the vertical ascription of praise is joined to the horizontal target of intention—"Glory to God in the highest, and on earth his peace for men."

I am reminded of the story of a certain downtown church which had a large, stained-glass window overlooking the busy High Street; across its face was the inscription: "Glory to God in the Highest." One day someone threw a stone at it and knocked out the *e* in

Highest, whereupon the inscription read: "Glory to God in the *High st.*"

Jesus was no hermit. No one ever accused him of being a spiritual introvert. How unsparingly he denounced the segregated ecclesiasticism and lopsided piety of the Pharisees! His arms embraced the sick and outcast—in a word, he spent his life in the service of others. From the "Highest" to the "High Street" is the scope of his religion—and ours, for

To worship rightly is to love each other.

But let one dimension be missing or become over-emphasized and true Christianity is distorted. The vertical may become monastic, mystical, and introspective, and the horizontal become a matter merely of human endeavor. We do well, then, to remember the unifying symbolism of the cross, and how, throughout his life, Jesus gave perfect expression of it. This truth comes to us again in some words of Karl Barth: "Man," he says, "is in vertical relation to God and in horizontal relation to his fellow men." Paul's answer to division in the church is to "preach Christ and him crucified," for by this event all men are made one.

"We have not really seen the cross of Christ," says Charles Koller, "until we have seen it as a great plus sign by which God and man are drawn together in holy reconciliation."

V

Symbolically, too, it is a nail which unites the old order and the new.

The cross has four compass points, and like an open scissors, all four extremities narrow to a central pivot. Imagine the cross as an X—like St. Andrew's cross. One angle takes us through the messianic hope of the Old Testament, and on into the life of our Lord until his death on the cross. The opposite angle continues the story from there, taking us on through the centuries.

For generations the Hebrews waited for Yahweh's Messiah; the waiting was long, and many, now dispersed among other nations and influenced by alien traditions, lost their vision. But however dark the times and long the delay, there remains a small nucleus of faithful people. The years narrow until one day in the town of Bethlehem the promised one is born. The waiting continues until he grows to manhood. He then emerges to call a group of men to be his disciples. As a result of his preaching and healing, he draws great crowds. But at the height of popularity he declares his intention to die on a cross.

From this moment many hopes are dashed. The angle narrows as crowds leave him. He spends most of his time with the Twelve, whose loyalty is by no means assured. At the final entry into Jerusalem it seems the angle is to narrow no further for the crowds are again with him; but his course is set. In the city he plans a meal with his only companions. Then it happens rapidly. One of them defects, and in the supreme moment of testing they all leave him—he is utterly alone.

When they fastened him to the cross, the angle reached its pivot. *But at the point where one angle ends, another begins.*

Easter morning dawns. First there is Mary Magdalene, then the other disciples. In the Upper Room the risen Lord once more meets his bewildered friends. They spend some time in his company, then he sends them out to be witnesses for him "in Jerusalem, Judea, Samaria, and away to the ends of the earth."

The angle widens very quickly. At Pentecost we read what sounds like an assembly of the United Nations. There is significance in this event, for though the new movement runs into severe trouble and many are put to death, God has endued it with power to overcome. As a result Christianity has now reached "the ends of the earth," leaping geographical limitations and political barriers.

And see how the beams of his cross point outward, ever wider—to infinity itself, for indeed, the church has not yet come of age, and the job of bringing the generations to his feet has only begun; yet however wide they extend and in whatever direction, they go back to that from which they are thrust out—*a nail in the center.*

At the utmost reach of both angles is the heart of Christianity, and like Paul, we proclaim Christ, nailed to the cross.

> *The powers of evil tried in vain;*
> *Hammer and nails had done their best*
> *Yet he is in the world again;*
> *In him all nations shall be blest.*

O Jesu, master, carpenter of Nazareth; who at the last upon the cross, through wood and nails didst purchase man's whole salvation; wield well thy tools in this thy workshop, that we who come to thee rough hewn may be fashioned to a truer beauty by thy hand; who ever liveth and reigneth with the Father and the Holy Spirit, one God, world without end. Amen.

7

THE RATTLE
of the DICE

After the crucifixion, the soldiers threw dice to divide up his clothes among themselves. Then they sat around and watched him as he hung there.

Matthew 27:35-36   The Living Bible

And sitting down they watched him there,
The soldiers did,
And while they played with dice
He made his sacrifice
To rid God's world of sin.
He was a gambler too, my Christ,
He took his life, threw it for a world redeemed,
And ere the westering sun went down,
Crowning that day with its golden crown,
He knew that he had won.

I

New Testament scholar Vincent Taylor reminds us that the garments of condemned prisoners were the perquisites of the soldiers who guarded the cross, and that these were divided by casting lots, "using the dice by which they whiled away the time."

"By which they whiled away the time." In other words, dicing for a victim's tunic was incidental. Perks or not, of what use were civilian clothes to a Roman Imperial soldier? All he could do would be to give them away or sell them for a denarius or two. So there were other reasons for carrying a dice. What were they?

I suggest two possibilities. The dice was either a means of escape from the horror of crucifixion or from its boredom.

Consider the first possibility. *The cross was shocking.* No form of execution ever gave its victim such pain, so that a bystander with but the slightest hint of compassion was bound to feel upset and in need of something to distract his mind.

As each Passion-tide approaches we hear the familiar story of Christ's sufferings, but could it be that we hear too easily and with little understanding? Listening from a church pew hardly takes us far enough; somehow we need to see and feel. I happen to think that devotional aids like crucifixes and Stations of the Cross are valuable in helping us enter the sorrows of our Lord. The free churches, of course, go more for hearing than seeing, thus laying a heavy responsibility on both preacher and listener. I feel that we need to be drawn closer and closer to the cross, for there in all its horror and wonder lies the hope of mankind.

When all is said and done, however, both in word and picture, we remain on the edge of a tremendous mystery—the love of God in Christ for sinful humanity. Jesus' suffering is really indescribable. But we are talking of more than physical pain. God laid on him his eternal purpose for the world; he bore the full weight of human sin and the destiny of men's souls. This was a burden that knows no parallel. In childlike simplicity we can but ponder and accept:

> *We may not know, we cannot tell,*
> *What pains he had to bear,*
> *But we believe it was for us*
> *He hung and suffered there.*

Though the depth of our Lord's sufferings remains unfathomable, nonetheless does the cross disturb us. This awful thing happened in our world and is part of our history, and though the years lengthen its timelag it remains timeless. Here somehow is the heart of all that matters, it haunts us and we are bound to investigate. Would that it were not so painful a task and that the cross had more pleasant aspects!

It has occurred to me that artists and sculptors never seem to portray Christ alive on the cross. It is always the dead Christ that we see, whose sufferings are over. If the intention was to show him in the midst of his sufferings, then the traditional motionless figure of Christ, almost in a state of blissful repose, fails to have meaning. Can it be indeed that traditional art has distorted the reality of the cross in attempting to make it less offensive to the onlooker?

The sculptor Maurice Roscini has at last ignored this approach. His magnificent work "Indifference" is based on the very occasion of our text. He shows

Christ alive on the cross, whose body writhes in terrible pain, while below are the two soldiers who dice for his garment. Roscini feels he has succeeded if people find its realism too hard to gaze upon, for this, he says, is how it is meant to be.

The cross is a repulsive thing, yet it is the heart of the Christian faith, and the effectiveness of our discipleship is dependent on our willingness to be part and parcel of the sufferings of the Savior. New Testament teaching is quite clear; Christians are called to deny themselves and take up the cross:

> *It is the way the Master went,*
> *Should not the servant tread it still?*

II

We salute the noble army of pioneers and martyrs of every age who have suffered for Christ. We honor their names who, in the propagation of the gospel and in the service of others, gave themselves without counting the cost.

But most of us want a break from that kind of thing— some place where we can "get away from it all," some occupation that will divert our attention. We wonder just how much we can stand.

And we have cause to wonder. This 20th century has been bloody and uncivilized—truly "red in tooth and claw." The "war to end all wars" was a pipedream, followed not by peace but by a brutal conflict that ravaged Europe and beyond, in which gas chambers and concentration camps were to reveal the most beastly and heinous aspect of man's nature.

Nor did it end there, for we are hard pressed to find any year since 1945 in which there has not been political and racial conflict somewhere.

The Vietnam war, the Nigerian-Biafran war, the Arab-Israeli war, the India-Pakistan war—to name but a few, have sapped the morale of millions as well as killed and maimed a multitude. Atrocities in Northern Ireland, mass anarchy, riots, strikes—all these we can watch nightly on television. By the nature of things, news is mostly bad news, with the result that we are constantly inundated with the horror side of life. Violence has reached such proportions as to constitute the world's greatest problem.

So it seems only human to turn one's face away, if only for a while, and try to forget. After all, can we really be expected to watch all the time? So we keep one hand on the escape-hatch—whatever it is that will take our minds off it—a good holiday, an evening at the local bar, a "show," the movies, the "races," football—anything, so long as it gets us away.

Who knows this better than the entertainment industry, the breweries, the drug-pushers? Drugs, drink, and sex all beckon man to turn his face away from whatever pains and frustrates him.

In Dr. Paul Tournier's book *The Healing of Persons* there is a chapter on "flight" in which the author examines man's search for escape. There is flight into dreams by which a person escapes from harsh reality into soothing fantasy. There is flight into the past in which a man walks away from present problems by turning his mind backwards. There is flight into the future by which utopian ideals also divert him from present realities. There is flight into disease by which a person can induce illness so as to escape a pressing demand or to acquire the sympathy of others. There is flight into passivity when life becomes completely negative and inactive. There is flight into work which—though in a way commendable—can also be a means of escape from pressing responsibilities. And there is flight into religion by which a man can become "too heavenly-minded to be of any earthly use."

There is some significance, it seems, in the fact that Paul Tournier's book, which was first published in 1940, should recently have been reprinted, for it speaks no less to our present day than it did to the bitter years in which it first appeared. There is war raging all around us, at one time in Africa, at another time in the Middle East or in the Far East. But war is not just open conflict between nations; war is internal—a country's own battle against corruption, dishonesty, and lawlessness, against the paralyzing effects of competitive greed. In this kind of war less blood may be shed, but it is no less an ugly spectacle, a sordid and brutal thing.

So it is not difficult to sympathize with those Roman soldiers. There were some, no doubt, who found themselves sensitive to the ghastly sight of crucifixion and who needed some distracting occupation while duty required them to keep watch. If dicing was their occupational therapy, who would deprive them of it?

As Christians we may sympathize but we cannot do likewise. We are people of the cross, and like Paul, we "bear in our bodies the marks of Jesus." We may long for the proverbial "wings of a dove" to take us away from the world's ugliness, but because we are committed to him who loved the world we have no escape from it.

In his book *The Lord's Prayer in Today's World*, Gerhard Ebeling writes about our idea that the devotional life bids us turn away from the world to God. "But what if God, to whom we turn in thus turning our back on the world, has himself not his back but his face to the world?"

Ronald Bryan, the Bengal bishop, relates in a poem the terrible hardship of life for many in India, made increasingly more difficult by mosquitoes, scorpions, spiders, white ants, and black ants. He is asking in effect who would want to live and work in such a place. He goes on to give a truly Christian answer:

> *In spite of all that you can say,*
> *If I'm allowed to have my way,*
> *I'll do my work and live my day*
> *In India still.*

III

On the other hand, did the soldiers play dice in order to escape boredom? Roman soldiers were trained hard and their training would more than likely curb personal emotions. Could it be that crucifixion was "just another job" that never taxed their minds and hearts, something they never really thought about? They were used to the sight of blood in their constant battles, and besides, crucifixions were "two-a-penny." So they play dice?

Matthew Arnold reminds us of that hard and pagan Roman world which, though it was cluttered with exciting things to see and do, yet

> *No easier nor no quicker passed*
> *The impracticable hours.*

Had the Roman become as bored with death as he was with life? This is really a frightening thought, for if "the worst death that man can die" had become a bore, then we have a streak in human nature which is both outrageous and terrifying. If it is in man to be so care-less and unmoved, what, we may ask, will he do or fail to do next?

In one of H. G. Wells's stories a certain Dr. Norbert expounds at some length on how civilization has brought with it all sorts of horrors and atrocities. A Mr. Frobisher eventually interrupts the dissertation by saying, "I don't care. The world may be going to pieces. The Stone Age may be returning. This may be as you say 'the sunset of civilization,' but I have other engagements. I am going to play croquet with my aunt at half-past twelve today."

Here is a perfect epitome of indifference. Everyman is challenged by the sorrows of his day. We may not have the sort of power to influence the course of world events, yet we are not powerless to pray, and the measure of our praying is the measure of our caring. We are faced today with dangers of such magnitude that the very existence of life on earth is threatened. But how much do we care? Do we heed man's cry for justice, his fight for human rights? Do we care about the world's millions bereft of food and shelter? And what of those cries for help and friendship in the place where we live—as close may be as our own doorstep?

Whatever else Jesus taught us, he taught us to care. Caring matters more than anything else.

Now the church, as we have seen, has not been without those great souls who gave their all in loving sacrifice; who refused "other engagements" for the primary task of caring in Christ's name. But in the same church there has existed, and still does, those who could not care less, or at least hardly ever show that they do. Nero is said to have fiddled while Rome burned, and this could well be the besetting sin of the church that it "traffics in triviality" while more important duties demand its attention: what J. B. Phillips calls "the lunatic topsyturvydom of many of our current values."

Kierkegaard remarked that he thought it was high time Christianity was taken away from men in order that they might appreciate it more. This may seem somewhat naive and exaggerated; nevertheless it is profoundly disturbing. There is nothing automatic about the continuance of any great and good thing, and it is not unknown for God to depart for a season so that men might be brought to their senses. Indeed the next hundred years could be more costly in blood, sweat, and tears for Christians, or for that matter for any who hold to a religious belief, than any time since the persecutions under the Roman Empire. The cross is ever beside us, waiting perhaps to bear us too.

Who then would dare to be a Christian? Let him know that he cannot avoid being tortured by human sin as Jesus was. Jesus demands that we get involved where it really hurts and where to bear witness is to suffer pain. Does he not then direct us to the hard, competitive world of industry, commerce, and technology, to trade unions and to the academic establishments of our land? If we do not stand up and be counted for Christ, others will be heard who bear disastrous philosophies. Will we spend our time, talent, and treasure on unimportant luxuries or will we forfeit these and every private triviality for the real cause of the kingdom? The church can do without the careless and apathetic, and there is no room in a caring society for Mr. Frobisher and his kind, for they bring upon us all the judgment of God.

"There is still time for nothing to happen," says Christopher Fry in one of his plays—and what an uncomfortable truth that is.

IV

It is time then to face facts and not to run from them. It is time to take Christ seriously and to realize the hard demands of our calling.

A Zen Buddhist is quoted as saying: "We think there is something in Christianity, but we don't think Christians know what it is."

Do we not believe that there was something—in fact everything in this man Jesus? He is Lord and King to whom we give unreserved loyalty. He is our authority in matters of faith and conduct. He is man yet more than man, for he is the Son of God and Savior of the world. He is perfect. He claims the following of every man and woman of every age.

Yet when once he was delivered into the hands of men and nailed to a cross, a couple of soldiers played dice at his feet. Here was the blackest and most decisive hour in world history, and what do we find?—men otherwise engaged; preoccupied with self-interest. And what if their little game be really escape from boredom, are we not faced with appalling human depravity?

Nor can we comfort ourselves by relegating this to the bad old days of ancient Rome before man's "coming of age." Today, tomorrow, someone surely will die—the victim of human hatred and human folly—so what? Who cares?

When Jesus came to Birmingham they simply passed him by,
They never hurt a hair by him, they only let him die;
For men had grown more tender, and they would not
*   give him pain,*
They only just passed down the street and left him in the
*   rain.*

G. A. Studdert Kennedy

Lord Jesus . . .
We have felt anger and shame that you were treated so
scandalously, so brutally; in our better moments we
say that we would not allow such things
*   to happen now . . .*
yet . . . men still fight wars . . .
civil strife has become part of our daily news . . .
the innocent suffer . . .
men, women, and children starve . . .
there is pain and agony caused by man's inhumanity to
man . . . so . . .
What are we to do, Lord?
Remind us again, for we forget so easily, of your words:
"I have set you an example; you are to do as I have
done for you."

8

THE CRY
of VICTORY

He said, "It is accomplished!" He bowed his head and gave up his spirit.   John 19:30

> Love's redeeming work is done,
> Fought the fight, the battle won:
> Lo! our sun's eclipse is o'er;
> Lo! He sets in blood no more.

I

When the battle of Waterloo ended the news was flashed by semaphore to London, and later the semaphore on Winchester cathedral began to repeat the message. Letter by letter it was spelled out: W–E–L–L–I–N–G–T–O–N D–E–F–E–A–T–E–D. . . . At that moment dense fog obliterated the semaphore. News of a lost battle quickly spread. Later in the day the fog cleared and the disconsolate people were overcome with joy as the semaphore arm moved again to spell out the complete message: W–E–L–L–I–N–G–T–O–N D–E–F–E–A–T–E–D T–H–E E–N–E–M–Y.

There was once another man whom many thought to be utterly defeated.

"We had been hoping that he was the man to liberate Israel."

"Crucified, dead, and buried," says the Apostles' Creed of him.

Some 30 years of preparation and three years of incredible activity—healing, preaching, and teaching—had ended in the most ignominious and conclusive way possible. Not that it was unexpected.

Jealous suspicion almost ended the life of the infant Christ, and when as a young man of 30 he returned to speak in his home town synagogue, folk took offense when he read from the Scriptures and inferred that he was the coming one they spoke of. They almost finished him there and then. That he lived for a couple of years through the malice that surrounded him is quite astonishing. His accusers hounded him persistently, hoping to force an admission of "messiahship." They caught him healing on the Sabbath, mixing with "tax-gatherers and sinners," talking to women and to hated Samaritans.

In their estimate he was everything that was wrong—dangerous radical, disturber of the status quo, law-breaker, blasphemer.

Small wonder he ended on a cross! And when his enemies saw him there and heard him cry out "It is accomplished," they surely congratulated one another.

"Got him at last! Now we can get on with the real business of our religion."

He was to them an upstart Messiah, but Christians believe and declare that he is the promised one, and that his messiahship is vindicated and not defeated by the cross; as Peter put it: "Let all Israel then accept as certain that God has made this Jesus, whom you crucified, both Lord and Messiah."

Not all can go that far. Some see him as a martyr—one in line with all other noble pioneers of reform who sealed their testimony with their blood. Others regard him as a good man—the best of men, whose only aim was to make people happy and more loving toward one another. Countless venerate him as "the greatest"—the supreme saint—teacher, preacher, healer, reformer "par excellence." But they have only gone part of the way. Christians assert the triumphant fact of Easter morning, and point to the living presence of Christ across 2000 years of history. Though it did appear that on Calvary Jesus had been defeated, the third day dawned to declare that instead he had defeated the enemy. Christ's resurrection gave his church impetus and inspiration to carry his truth through the centuries. His resurrection has enabled the church to withstand the "slings and arrows of outrageous fortune." Christian worship is not a memorial service to a dead hero, but an expression in praise and prayer of the "accomplishment" of Christ, and a reminder to the world that he is alive in it.

Nor is the church a tomb. Said a sceptic recently: "God is dead, and the church is his tombstone." Granted, this impression is too often given, but it totally denies the New Testament affirmation that "God who raised Jesus from the dead" is best seen and known in him. Stanley Jones tells of a Muslim who taunted a Christian, saying that whereas they had the tomb of their prophet as a place of pilgrimage, the Christians had no certain burial place which they knew to be the tomb of Jesus. Instantly came the reply: "We have no tomb because we have no corpse."

II

No martyr, no tomb, no corpse—what then are we to say of this man who was nailed to a cross and laid in a grave, and what can be the significance of his final words—for a person's last words are thought to be significant? We should listen intently to what a dying man has to say, for not only is it a comfort for him to be able to communicate, but we may also learn a great deal about him which perhaps we never knew or had misunderstood before. Our hopes and fears are never more to the fore than when we stand on the brink of the "Great Beyond."

Two bandits were crucified with Jesus. Luke tells us that one died with taunts and abuses on his lips, but the other, acknowledging his guilt alongside the innocence of Jesus, repented.

"I tell you this," said Jesus, "today you shall be with me in paradise." Not even his own suffering unto death prevented the outreach of his redeeming love.

A soldier in one of Studdert Kennedy's dialect poems finds it incredible that Jesus should want to forgive his executors:

> Mind ye, I'm not sure I likes it; I'm for giving
>   what ye gets—
> I'm for strikin' back as 'ard as you've been struck.
> But I just couldn't do it,
> I'd bust, and blind, and blue it;
> 'Tain't the prayin' as I'm gone on—it's the pluck.

But in the final words of the dying Christ there is no retaliation, no curses, only love and faith and triumph. Ignace Lepp remarked: "Those who learn to face death with greatest calm are those who love life with the most zest." Such befits our Lord.

"It is accomplished," he said. Many, no doubt, said the same—his disciples back at their fishing nets, and all his friends who believed he really was the Messiah; the Roman soldiers who had completed another crucifixion; the Jewish authorities with a sigh of relief; and the cynics with a "hard-lines-old-chap" attitude.

But Jesus did not mean it this way. He is not admitting defeat—as if to say, "I've done my best and I'm sorry for having failed." Nor is it a sigh of relief that death has come at last to bring release from his awful pain. *It is a cry of victory* that his task is complete and he can confidently leave the outcome in the hands of his Father, God.

Earlier he had told his disciples that it was his meat and drink "to do the will of him who sent me until I have finished his work," and in his great prayer he says, "I have glorified thee on earth by completing the work which thou gavest me to do."

It was the most colossal piece of work ever allotted to one man, and its chance of success was fraught with the most impossible odds, *but he brought it off*, and there was no flaw in any part of it; indeed, words fail to describe its magnificence and to estimate its worth:

> *O perfect life of love,*
> *Ali, all is finished now;*
> *All that he left his throne above*
> *To do for us below.*

"It is accomplished," and by this he meant that one chapter in his autobiography had ended, but far from its being his "last will and testament," he intended that it should be followed shortly by the next chapter. He said that he would be crucified and be raised again on the third day, so that "the third day" would see the beginning of this new chapter, and it would be continuous, volume after volume, world without end.

So after reading in one place the final words of the dying Christ, we go on to read not his obituary but the astounding news of his return to life. And it really was a return, for he was once more engaged in the tasks he had previously performed—calling, reassuring, reconciling. To say that his "accomplishment" had begun again is to sound illogical and to contradict the laws of language, but this is the amazing fact of the resurrection. I accept on the one hand the argument that the resurrection was not so much a miracle as the only thing God could do to vindicate his purpose, so that it would have been illogical not to have happened; yet I stagger before the sheer wonder that it *did* happen and that the powers of evil did not win. I feel prone to call it "divine inconsistency," for if God ever defies logic, this is it. That the cross— "a stumbling-block to Jews and folly to Greeks"— should become God's universal symbol of glory and way of salvation, is sheer miracle.

And it is a continuous miracle, for while human schemes rise and fall, his "scheme" is eternal and unstoppable. He wends his way through the vicissitudes of men, pioneering, reforming, calling, challenging, comforting, and healing.

John Masefield speaks of this in his play about

our Lord's death and resurrection. Pontius Pilate's wife, Procula, is greatly interested in Jesus and is anxious to prevent Pilate sending him to his death. She calls for the centurion who had been in charge of the crucifixion, and who had confessed Jesus as "a Son of God." His name was Longinus. Procula asks him what had happened at the crucifixion. "He was a fine young fellow," he answered, "but when we had done with him, he was a poor, broken-down thing, dead on the cross."

"Do you think he is dead?" said Procula.

"No, lady," replied Longinus, "I don't."

"Then where is he?" asked Procula.

"Let loose in the world, lady, where neither Roman nor Jew can stop his truth."

There are two ways at least in which the release of the victorious Christ into all the world has had effect. The one is in *victorious living* and the other in *victorious dying*.

III

Jesus enables us to live victoriously.

See a group of frightened, bewildered disciples, convinced that it was all over, now being knit into the nucleus of a world church. Peter their leader is converted for good. Says Murdo Macdonald: "Jesus took the shifting sands of Peter's character and turned them into granite."

And there is Paul the great apostle who many times might have admitted defeat. Battered and bruised for his faith, in and out of prison and expecting death at any time, yet to persecute and chain him is not to stop him. Lock him up and he turns his imprisonment into an opportunity to further the gospel, and if he cannot preach in prison then he will write from prison. In one of his confinement letters he says: "I wish you to know that what has happened to me has really served to advance the gospel." Such is the spirit of Christ in men, who, when all seemed lost, went on to conquer.

Beethoven suffered most of his life from a liver disease. Then came what to a composer and musician is the worst of tragedies—deafness. Defeat stared him in the face but he refused to go under, and it is a remarkable testimony that most of his great works were written when he was unable to hear a note. He was very conscious of the help of one beyond himself.

Then there was George Frederick Handel. All his life he was dogged by misfortune; debt followed debt; despair followed despair. A cerebral hemorrhage paralyzed his right side and for four years he could neither walk nor write. Doctors gave him up, but he revived to write several operas, only to be plunged once more into deep debt. Nearing sixty he felt finished. "Why did God permit my resurrection only to allow my fellow men to bury me again? Why did he vouchsafe a renewal of my life if I may be no longer permitted to create? My God, my God, why hast thou forsaken me?" Then when all seemed lost, he was challenged by a poet friend Charles Jennens to write "a sacred oratorio." Reading the Scriptures and finding in the sufferings of the Savior an affinity with his own, he went to work. For 24 days without eating a crumb, he worked like a fiend to produce "Messiah"—which many consider the greatest oratorio ever written. His accomplishment lives on.

There was a man "dug in" on the beaches of Normandy in the June of 1944. He had seen two beautiful

Norman churches badly damaged by tank gunfire, and this grieved him terribly, for he was an architect. "What are you going to do when all this is over?" asked a fellow soldier, and Basil Spence replied: "Build a cathedral." Four years earlier, the lovely Coventry cathedral had been laid in a heap of ruins following one night's terrible bombing. Today a fine modern cathedral of his planning has arisen from the rubble of the old, and at the heart of the old, a reminder of Christ on his cross—"Father, forgive."

Many times it seemed like the end for Martin Luther King. Beaten up, stabbed in the chest, his home bombed—yet not once did he admit defeat. Though he died of an assassin's bullet, his "accomplishment" continues in the dream that one day there will be victory for the righteous and peace among all races.

Such is their faith, and such their reasons for it. To see these men triumph over crippling circumstances is to see the cross on the world's stage and the drama of the crucifixion reenacted before our eyes. It is to see defeat stared at and defied, to hear the cry "accomplished" not as resignation but as conquest.

Jesus gave himself for us and gives himself to us so that we might live victoriously, overcoming evil with good and failure with faith.

IV

And he helps us to die victoriously.

In his book *Faith in a Secular Age*, Colin Williams tells of some negroes who in 1964 went to the site of the first slave market in Florida to commemorate the tercentenary of the landing there of slaves brought to the U.S.A. During the rally they were surrounded by angry whites who threatened them with guns. It seemed that death would come to them at any moment, but they continued undaunted. When one of the leaders was asked why they risked death he replied that it was because they believed in the resurrection.

Death is the great hush-up. It is said to have replaced sex as the unmentioned, unmentionable taboo of our culture. We are said either to joke inappropriately and uncomfortably about it, or else to overdramatize it. Blaise Pascal spoke a truth for our day: "We spend all our lives trying to take our minds off death." Still others have spoken of death as "the dreaded extinguisher of life's little candle"; "the conqueror of the self we have so carefully preserved"; "the unwanted guest at our last supper bringing to an end our eating and merry-making."

But whoever accepts the death and resurrection of Jesus should never feel this way. Jesus has put the world in his debt, for who can ever repay him, not just for dying and rising, but for what he did to death itself? He changed its image as a cruel monster into a means of grace. For him it was a fundamental fact of life. Life was really about dying. He said that if any man sought to save his life he would lose it, but that whoever should lose his life would preserve it.

The marvel of his teaching is that death is not extinction but fulfillment; not a catastrophe but an accomplishment. He saw death as a gateway to a greater life, and that we are willingly to give up what we have in order to receive something better. What God has prepared for those who love him rightly remains beyond our knowledge, but we can be sure it is the culmination of a process already begun. In fact, to accept Christ here is to be in possession of it, for "he who puts his faith in the Son has hold of eternal life." Christians believe that Jesus not only passed through death but that he conquered it and gives it as a gift.

What then holds terror for the Christian? Paul is sure that nothing in the whole creation can tear us apart from God's love in Christ. "In spite of all," he says, "overwhelming victory is ours through him who loved us."

Origen in A.D. 248, seeing that the most terrible persecution was about to break out upon the church—and it did two years later—said: "Every religion will be overthrown and that of the Christian's will alone prevail. It is not only possible, but literal truth, that all the inhabitants of Asia, of Europe, and of Africa, Greeks and Barbarians to the world's end, every soul of man, shall come to agreement under the law of Christ."

Call this presumptuous and impossible, nevertheless it is Christianity's assignment. The living Christ has in triumph accomplished one chapter, yet the world is far from his design for it, and there is work to be done "while men go suffering, sinning, still."

> But an empty tomb is waiting, and the East is
>   silver grey,
> As the angels of the morning trumpet in another day,
> See the wounded God go walking down the world's
>   eternal way,
>   For his task is never done.
>   G. A. Studdert Kennedy